What Remains to Be Said

Also by
Robert B. Shaw

POETRY

A Late Spring, and After (2016)

Aromatics (2011)

Solving for X (2002)

Below the Surface (1999)

The Post Office Murals Restored (1994)

The Wonder of Seeing Double (1988)

Comforting the Wilderness (1977)

CRITICISM

Blank Verse: A Guide to its History and Use (2007)

The Call of God: The Theme of Vocation in the Poetry of Donne and Herbert (1981)

AS EDITOR

Henry Vaughan: Selected Poems (1976)

American Poetry since 1960: Some Critical Perspectives (1973)

What Remains to Be Said

New and Selected Poems

by

Robert B. Shaw

PINYON PUBLISHING
Montrose, Colorado

Copyright © 2022 by Robert B. Shaw

All rights reserved. Except as permitted under the U.S. Copyright Act of 1976, no part of this publication may be reproduced, distributed, or transmitted in any form or by any means, or stored in a database or retrieval system, without the prior written permission of the publisher, except for brief quotations in articles, books, and reviews.

Cover Art: "The Open Book" by Juan Gris, 1925

Oil on canvas, 73 cm x 92 cm, Kunstmuseum Bern, Switzerland.

Photograph of Robert B. Shaw by Hilary A. Shaw

First Edition: April 2022

Pinyon Publishing
23847 V66 Trail, Montrose, CO 81403
www.pinyon-publishing.com

Library of Congress Control Number: 2022930142
ISBN: 978-1-936671-84-7

ACKNOWLEDGMENTS

Some poems in the first section of this book have appeared in the following publications:

Alabama Literary Review: "Postal Pieces," "Around the Block," "Muscle Man," "Devices"

Literary Matters: "A Cloud Shadow," "Leonardo's Vitruvian Man"

Pinyon Review: "For Gary Entsminger," "My Mother's Hundredth Birthday," "Note from a New Address," "In the Kitchen," "Wants and Needs"

Woven Tale Press: "Enigmas of Weeding," "Daytime Moon," "*Lacrimae Rerum*"

For selections from previously published books, credits are as follows:

"Boston Sunday Dinner," "Gargoyle," "Jack-O'-Lantern," "A Study," "From Ashes," "Snake Crossing," "In Witness," "The Pause," "Grass Widows," and "Another Day" from *Comforting the Wilderness* © 1977 by Robert B. Shaw. Published by Wesleyan University Press. Used by permission.

Poems from *The Wonder of Seeing Double* (University of Massachusetts Press, 1988), reprinted by permission of the author.

Poems from *The Post Office Murals Restored* (1994) and *Below the Surface* (1999), reprinted by permission of Copper Beech Press.

Poems from *Solving for X* (2002), reprinted by permission of Ohio University Press.

Poems from *Aromatics* (2011) and *A Late Spring, and After* (2016), reprinted by permission of Pinyon Publishing.

Contents

Foreword   1

NEW POEMS (2022)

Morning Song   5
Enigmas of Weeding   6
Leap Day   7
March 20   8
A Cloud Shadow   9
Note from a New Address   10
Daytime Moon   11
After the Latest Mass Shooting   12
In the Kitchen   13
Lacrimae Rerum   14
Devices   15
Night after Night   17
Wants and Needs   17
Things They Left Behind   20
My Mother's Hundredth Birthday   21
Around the Block   24
A Mantel Clock   26
After the Fact   27
For Gary Entsminger   28
Leonardo's Vitruvian Man   29
Muscle Man   31

The Restive Retiree   33
Postal Pieces   34
Later Life   36
Library Gnomes   38
The Tetragrammaton   40
Teaching Poetry   41
Postscript Ahead of Time   42

FROM *COMFORTING THE WILDERNESS* (1977)

Boston Sunday Dinner   45
Gargoyle   46
Jack-O'-Lantern   47
A Study   48
From Ashes   50
Snake Crossing   51
In Witness   52
The Pause   53
Grass Widows   54
Another Day   55

FROM *THE WONDER OF SEEING DOUBLE* (1988)

Narcissus   59
Echo   60
Family Album   61
Bright Enough to See Your Face In   62

To the Cricket   64
Extended Run   65
The Shortcut   66
Contemporary Music   67
Old Burying Ground   69
Chronometrics   70
Partial Draft   73
Homework   74
There and Back Again   75
The Voice of the Yawn   77
Safe Harbor   78
Spring's Awakening   79
The Floater   80
The Invention of Zero   80
Their Voices   81
Ash Wednesday, Late Afternoon   82
A Time Piece   83
Morning Exercise   84
Just Here and Now   85

FROM *THE POST OFFICE MURALS RESTORED* (1994)

Serving the Purpose   89
Degrees of Resolution   89
A Piece of Rope   91
At the Bait Store   93
Camera Obscura   95
Fanlight   96
Last Days in Camden   97

Shut In   103
Picturesque   105
The Bookmark   105
A Pair of Bookends   106
An Aspen Grove   107
Again, Cicadas   108
Monarchs   109
Lunar Eclipse   111
The Leaning Tree   112
A Record Price   113
December Vespers   114
To His Pulse   115
The Key   116
Florilegium   117
Advanced Research   119
Finding the Diary   121
Wind at Night   124
The Post Office Murals Restored   125

FROM *BELOW THE SURFACE* (1999)

Paper Birch   137
12:00 M   138
Backyard Archeology   138
These Days   140
Low Tide   142
On the Footbridge   143
Halfway   144
On a Birthday   145

Getting Farsighted   146
Old Address Book   147
Night Lights   148
Man with Metal Detector   149
Proscenium Masks   152
A Mica Mine   153
An Exhumation   155
The Crayons   158
Time-Lapse Photography   160
The Porch Swing   161
Hide-and-Seek   162
On Their Anniversary It Rained   164
Ice Time   165
Specimen Starfish   166
First Bird   167
Another Orpheus   168
A Geode   170
Cave   172
In the Rear-View Mirror   175

FROM *SOLVING FOR X* (2002)

The Future Perfect   179
Back Again   180
Airs and Graces   180
A Field of Goldenrod   182
Anthology Piece   183
The End of the Sonnet   184
Dec. 23   184
The Devil's Garden   186

Waiting Room   187
The Arbor   188
A Roadside Flock   188
"Called Back"   190
Up and Away   191
Drowned Towns   192
Snowplow in the Night   198
Espalier   199
Solving for X   199
Ant in Amber   201
Wishing Well   201
A Flashback   202
Letter of Recommendation   203
Out of Character   204
Making Do   205
Pilgrims   207
Other Eyes   208
QWERTY   210
A Drained Fountain   211

FROM *AROMATICS* (2011)

Wild Turkeys   215
The Odometer   216
Aromatics   217
Tantalus   220
A New Life   221
The Better Part of Valor   222
Iridescence   224
Butterfly at the Beach   225

What She Found   227
Oak Leaves in Winter   228
Memory   229
Habit   230
The Poe Toaster Prepares for His Annual Visit   231
A Spirit Photograph: W. B. Yeats and Another   233
Questions about Elizabeth Bishop's Clavichord   235
Old Man of the Mountain   237
Working Out   238
Thresholds   240
Hill Towns in Winter   241
Parable of the Birds   243
One Black Squirrel   244
River and Road   245
In Storage: A Calder Cat   247
Thirst at Midnight   248
A Certain Other Slant   249
Sundial in the Rain   250
Blue Period Sketch   251
Dusk   253

FROM *A LATE SPRING, AND AFTER* (2016)

I. *VESSEL*

My First Atlas   257
Craquelure   259
Selection   261
Handiwork   262

Wear   263
A Beacon   265
The Custody of the Eyes   266
Cézanne: "The House with the Cracked Walls"   267
Vessel   268

II. *NOW WE NOTICE*

Dinosaur Tracks   270
Belligerents   271
"Pity the Monsters!"   273
The House of the Tragic Poet   274
Lachrymatory   276
On the Death of Wilmer Mills   277
A Confirmation   278
September Toadstools   279
Winter Stars   280
Hanging On   281
An Arrangement of Dried Flowers   282
Now We Notice   283

III. *A LATE SPRING, AND AFTER*

The Tally   284
What Happened   286
A Late Spring   289
The Loss of the Joy of Cooking   290
Voicemail   291
Your Hand   292
Clockwork Sonnet   293
The Sun Room Plants   294
Fluid Ounces   294

Through a Glass, Darkly   295
Afterthought   296
Eight Months Later   297
Envoy   298

IV. *FERRYING*

By the Pond   298
Paths Crossing   300
News Item   300
Sensitive Plant   302
Her Mother's Seashell   303
Transformation Scene   304
Ferrying   305
Winter Sunset   307

Notes   311

FOREWORD

The earliest poem reprinted in this book was written in 1966, when I was nineteen. Most of the new poems in the first section were written over a period of about a year bridging 2020 and 2021. I leave it to others to do the math; clearly, though, I have reached a point suitable for some self-assessment and the winnowing that goes with it.

In reprinting poems from my seven published volumes, I have made only a few changes: regularizing punctuation and spelling, correcting a printer's error in one case, and in another smoothing out a metrical bump that has bothered me for decades. Otherwise, I have left the texts alone. In regard to poems written by an earlier self, sometimes many years ago, I believe later thoughts are not necessarily going to be better ones. Poems about which I have serious doubts have simply been set aside. While making my selection I sometimes came upon pieces which I had no quarrel with, but which struck me as overlapping too closely in theme or in subject matter with some I planned to include; and these also I have omitted, in the interest of minimizing dilution.

Usually my hope is that my poems will not require glossing (at least by me). In a few instances, though, I have supplied notes on subjects or sources which may be unfamiliar to some readers.

I have retained the dedications that appeared in the previously published volumes. The section of new poems carries its own dedication. Toward the people named in those inscriptions, whether living or dead, my feelings of thankfulness and affection are immeasurable.

R. B. S.

New Poems (2022)

For Peggy R. Ellsberg,
admired writer, enduring friend

MORNING SONG

The songs I wake to hear
are songs unbound to words.
Through darkness, sweet and clear,
arise the notes of birds

who beg the day to break
in answer to their plea.
They want the sun to wake.
Why not? They wakened me.

Now, at the eastern edge
of all-surrounding night,
a red and widening wedge
of long-awaited light

splits dark apart and wins
their chorus of hoorays,
leads on the sun, begins
the latest of their days.

The dark outside, the deeper
dark behind the eyes,
depart and rouse the sleeper
with them to harmonize.

They never fail to render
thanks for the vital gift,
the daystar pouring splendor
on all life—slow and swift,

some wordless, others able
to utter praise in words.
Here at the kitchen table

I second what the birds

have offered up in praises:
Once more, the sun, the sun!
The miracle amazes
every time it's done.

ENIGMAS OF WEEDING

Wading into my garden's anarchy,
I see it little matters where I start.
The rubber kneeling pad I have with me,
the slender, pointed trowel can't do their part

till I, as sponsoring intelligence,
decide what needs to go from this small jungle.
With so much up for grabs, I feel as dense
as stalks I'm dealing with, and bound to bungle.

I'm never sure if one's a weed or not.
Ragweed, all right, but more nefarious
masters of masquerade have clearly got
an edge, so good are they at flaunting various

crafty facsimile leaves adorning stems
equally plausible (though look, that one's
fuzzier, isn't it?). Their stratagems
entrench them so nearby authentic ones

that picking out ersatz from genuine
is scarcely judgment, more like throwing dice.

Camouflage breached, as tangled clumps grow thin
and plots grow neater, real plants pay a price.

I think of seedling patterns I designed
whose sprouts too soon gave ground to bastard brothers.
And now, with both so thickly intertwined,
ripping out some will have to uproot others.

No doubt it's worth it for the ones remaining—
more light, more air for each, and more expanse
to siphon water from each time it's raining.
The good ones that are gouged out by mischance,

like phrases tried and dropped from poems like this,
are not at fault, just lodged in the wrong place,
I tell myself. A kneeling nemesis,
I drudge away. Sweat irrigates my face.

It will take time to see if this day's culling
was what the larger look of things required.
Parsing dubious shoots, perplexed, kept mulling,
this weeder's growing well and truly tired.

LEAP DAY

How to interpret this interpolation?
Sidling in at the end of the stunted month,
February, which no one could want more of,
rousted each fourth year out of hibernation,
this stepchild of the calendar tenders back
those hours that go for three years overlooked as

our planet less than neatly circles the sun.

Another day capped with a low cloud ceiling,
floored by snow resisting a merger with mud,
decidedly not for picnics or parades—
the calendar needs it, but do we? As long
as it's on offer, we'll most likely take it.
Tomorrow and tomorrow and tomorrow …
We answer spellbound to a daily order
drummed deep into us, infiltrating our cells:
Forward, March. Just so. Ignore the obvious:
each day's job lot of steps brings closer a day
when just getting up from bed could seem like a leap.

MARCH 20

Two sumo wrestlers in a ring—
Winter is one, the other, Spring—
conduct their semi-annual bout,
straining to shove each other out.
They heave and grunt, blow hot and cold,
act as if nothing's been foretold.
A single dwindling patch of snow
hints at how, this time, things will go:
cold nights are scripted to give way
to warmth with every lengthened day.

Granted, our storm-bedraggled yard
makes a confidence a little hard
to come by, though we know, in fact,
the match is fixed, the deck is stacked.

Why else would lately altered clocks
pay homage to the equinox?
The balance tips to green from white.
Advancing day eclipses night.
Our planet's tilt is set on it.
Thank Heaven, we can bet on it.

A CLOUD SHADOW

By this time in the spring
the hillside's buried green
is mostly resurrected:
a wide and grassy screen
on which is now projected
this dark amorphous thing.

Like some untidy blotch
a giant Holstein shed
from off its hide while grazing—
the thought could fill a head
straining for some amazing
phenomenon to watch.

With the same sight to ponder,
another, though, might think
how Chinese seers would train
rapt eyes on pools of ink
to see the future plain.
Downcast and slow to wander,

the shadow seems to brood

on our attempts to tame it
as well as we are able,
to pin it down and name it.
Drifting, unstable, sable,
it shirks similitude.

NOTE FROM A NEW ADDRESS

This house I moved to just last summer
sits on a ridge whose chief renown
I learned of as a green newcomer:
"Goddam windiest place in town."

Weather, disarming, can be quiet
down in the flats, while that up here
will stir and ache to start a riot,
ready to race and domineer.

Drafted from that same reservoir
out of which common breath is drawn,
it bellows like a tidal bore
as it comes punishingly on.

Air is delightful, but when charging
hellbent and howling in one's face …?
Then the opinion needs enlarging.
Air is delightful—in its place.

Wind alone, though, is not to blame:
the ridge, its topographic crony,
riles it up to play their game.

Shingles torn off bear testimony.

I wish these gusts would wane in strength;
I know my wish is not the ridge's.
It means, through all its crested length,
to take the air, and not by smidges.

Tuned by the ridge's shifting levels,
wind ravens on. What more to say?
Memo to earth- and air-borne devils:
Having moved in, I mean to stay.

DAYTIME MOON

When I was a child, an out-of-phase moon
was a puzzle at first, then a pitiful sight:
out shuffling dazed through the blue afternoon—
why couldn't the moon tell the day from the night?

It's not any less haggard at this later date.
I see it hung low at the end of the street,
lackluster and listless, a much-scoured plate,
a target for anyone targeting skeet.

The hours we keep it appears not to heed,
like a lamp staying on from the evening before,
too late or too early to answer a need.
Where's the switch for on / off? It has just either / or.

I suppose, on reflection (and let it be stated,
reflection is what gives to moonlight its bounce),

its mood of malaise fits our fear of what's fated,
our feeling of waiting for something to pounce.

After any old dismal terrestrial stuff
it once had to be sad about when I was small,
these days of contagion are more than enough
to keep its worn chalky face white as a pall.

Here and now, in and under a chilly spring sky,
as we contemplate what the Fourth Horseman will bring,
we renew our acquaintance, the day moon and I,
with no end near at hand to our grim witnessing.

May 2020

AFTER THE LATEST MASS SHOOTING

The motto's changed: Live free *and* die.
No time for us to wonder why,
as each new rabid burst of rage
brings politicians to the stage
to fill a slot in that day's news
by nattering their threadbare views.
They hope the Public understands:
the Constitution ties their hands.
And anyway, no statute can
forestall an armed and angry man
who wants to show what he resents
by slaughtering some innocents.
They sign off then with "thoughts and prayers"

before returning to their lairs.

Thoughts: how blame can be deflected.
Prayers: for getting re-elected.

IN THE KITCHEN

You'll never know what made your grip on the glass
fumble as you picked it up from the counter
to set it on the shelf, but fumble it did,
and now the glass has left you empty-handed,
slipping or almost springing away from you
as though on a suicide mission no one
could ever expect from such an uncomplaining
homely half-pint. Your eyes lock on its progress
downward, in seeming slow motion, tensing you
to feel what's irreversible all the more
sharply, as you wait for the stone kitchen floor
to smash it into pieces upon impact.
The sound, when it comes, is the inanimate
equivalent of a doomed, ultimate shriek.
Look, on the tiles: a slew of fragments that seem
enough in quantity to make two or three
such tumblers at least, and in shapes and sizes
ranging from shards to splinters to smithereens—
to scarcely visible mites of jaggedness.
An inexpensive, not so easy to chip
bit of glassware: who would have thought a modest
vessel could so encapsulate, so unleash
catastrophe accomplished in an instant?
You never gave it much appreciation

earlier; maybe now it will have startled
out of you some respect as an exemplum—
suggesting what? That you should be more careful?
As a lifelong belt-and-suspenders person
you don't find that enlightening. No, it's more
a reminder of how close behind the scrim
of your placid day-to-day sense of safety
chaos waits to occasionally poke through.
Yes. That is what this brokenness says to you.

LACRIMAE RERUM

Up too early the morning after a night
of widely scattered sleep, just barely awake,
I skimmed a bookseller's latest catalogue
offering vintage volumes of poetry,
some of them autographed. Beneath one title
by someone I once knew, my tired eyes halted
partway through the description, snagged by the words
"small tears." Well, yes, I thought, that's a fair enough
way to define the mood of this maker's work:
the effects of loss, of yearnings unfulfilled
encoded in still ponds and withered leaves,
subdued regrets summed up in misty landscapes.
No blatancy, no histrionic keening,
just a dignified undertone of sadness,
a Virgilian tinge. Then I finished my tea,
and looked more closely at the page and realized
the words referred to rips in the dust jacket.

I know: a stupid way to begin the day.
Still, was my misreading all that misleading?
Think of the small tears (rhyming with years) distilled
into those pensive lines. Think of the small tears
(rhyming with cares) that aging will instigate,
insidious fissures in the once unmarred
jacket, beckoning dust to find a way in.
I should remember not to read at breakfast,
given there's all the time in the world to note
how persuasively these two manage to blur
together—the tears of things, the tears in things.

DEVICES

In '40s movies that our parents watched
this was a standard scene: an empty room
which someone had just left or not yet entered,
and on the table a black telephone
ringing away with no one to pick up.
A plot device to send lives off the rails:
She will not learn that he is still alive.
He will not know that she's forgiven him.
She will assume he's gone for good to Burma.
He will believe her parents have succeeded
in poisoning her mind against his pleadings.
The phone stops ringing. News does not get through.
They and all others doomed by such bad timing
head for the wars or marry the wrong people,
and end up suffering for most of the film.

That black phone with its black snake of a cord

(one thinks of Henry Ford's first Model Ts:
"Any color they want as long as it's black")
updated earlier calamitous
miscarriages of tidings: lagging couriers
leaving Romeo and Juliet
to blunder through sequential suicides;
as well as countless intercepted letters
destroyed through malice or possessiveness,
adding an easy poignancy to novels
(novels, of course, from when we still wrote letters).

But now these tragedies of happenstance
are lost to us. Shrunk and minus its cord
the phone goes with us now, snug in a pocket,
vibrating as though with its own pulse.
There is no way for us to miss connection,
no way to evade it if we wished.
The good and bad news find us where we are;
the old excuse of being uninformed,
however tempting, can't now be believed.
Breakups happen, but the couples trade
remote reproaches while they walk through airports,
make their own mess without the folderol
of interfering relatives conspiring.
We got so tired of being out of the loop
we've made the loop our daily route to plod.
Can it be phones feel free without their cords?
How free do we feel, tied to our devices
which are different, but not different enough
from what the Prayer Book, soberly probing, calls
the devices and desires of our hearts?

NIGHT AFTER NIGHT

Later, and much too late for it to make
a difference in the way that things turned out,
one image kept him helplessly awake,
his mind pinned down, his body tossed about:
a phone, left sitting dormant on its table.
(Phones were tied down with cords back then, of course.)
If he had used it, would he have been able
to counteract the nameless, sudden force
that unforeseen had wrenched her from his reach?
(Stunned, he had felt that next the sky might fall.)
Could he have won her over with a speech,
curbing his pride enough to make the call?
Such thinking wasn't totally a dumb thing.
There was a time he might have altered something.

WANTS AND NEEDS

When my father's mother was pressed to give up
her tiny apartment and move out to live
with one of her daughters in the country, she
made it obvious how she felt about it
before, during, and after relocation.
My father would explain: "She's okay, really.
Except … she just wants to be ten years younger,
and live in New York City, and walk through stores
without buying anything, and go to lunch
someplace like Stouffer's, where she would be able
to start conversations with strangers sitting

near to her, if they seem to be nice enough."
He might have added other peaceful pastimes:
library visits, museum talks, long strolls
down New York sidewalks where she might see someone
like Mrs. Roosevelt getting out of a cab.
Nothing extravagant, then—just all of it
impossible. Her life as an elderly,
neat-as-a-pin *flâneuse* had to be kindly
but firmly shelved.

                Even when such innocent
routines were something she could handle, nothing
quite diffused the underlying anxiousness
she brought along like invisible luggage
on weekend visits, setting children on edge,
puzzling grownups, making the air prickle
with nervousness and guilt. Passive aggression,
I learned to call it when I grew up. Her way
of padding past my father, deep in the *Times*,
asking, "Is there any news in the paper?"
Her insistence that her weak tea was never
weak enough ("Dishwater," an uncle jeered).
Her flurried interjections—"Excuse, excuse!"—
highlighting things that no one would have noticed,
or, if noticed, thought needed their excusing.
Her almost manic coddling of small children,
forcing on them peppermints from her handbag,
dabbing off smudgy tear-streaks from their faces
with one of many scallop-edged handkerchiefs.
She couldn't settle down; her circulating
from room to room was like a weathered fragment
of flotsam swirling round in a slow eddy.

Something must have been missing that she sought for,
sensing the gap without ever pinning down
what plagued her with it. Was it her mother's death,

early on, the stepmother she took leave of
as soon as she was of age? Was it the Church,
that *cast her out* (so the murmured story went)
for marrying our Protestant grandfather?
Was she just a wanderer, or a pilgrim?
Her dips into religion were eclectic
by the time I was old enough to notice:
midweek drop-ins at dimlit midtown churches,
mostly Episcopal, not for services,
but just to rest a few minutes in a pew
on her way home from some free lecture somewhere.
It probably was calming, maybe even
inspiring, like the stack of slender books
by Kahlil Gibran hallowing her nightstand.

Were there still lingering reverberations
of her strange late-in-life separation from
her husband after bringing up five children?
Living apart, but seemingly on good terms,
never a cross word between them when
they overlapped at family occasions;
every few months when he was back in New York
for a board meeting, he would take her to lunch
at (a bit daring for her) The House of Chan.
None of the relatives could understand it.
Speculation was just that: speculation.
And since the yen for privacy that bound them
was like a blood-oath, they didn't speak of it.

Children settled, grandchildren growing, for years
at the YWCA she took in
a modest salary tending the front desk,
enough to live on back then in the '50s,
even to fund her inexpensive pleasures.
Of course, it couldn't last; she came to the point
of wanting what my father said she wanted,

the things that age and ebbing health stole from her.

She was well cared for when she could no longer
care for herself. She faded away gently,
leaving her mysteries dangling as wispy
denizens of memory's mothballed closet.
She wanted her ashes flung from boat or plane
out beyond the Atlantic's ten-mile limit,
which was, everyone agreed when the time came,
simply not practical. So that was one more
wish unrequited.

        The list of things we want
can write itself. It only ever meshes
unevenly with the list of things we get.
Most grow used to the mismatch. But what about
the things we *need*? For those, is it our failing
to find them names that kindles our restlessness,
sending us out to drag our captive shadows
in slow, tightening circles while remaining
blinkered, somehow, to what it is that goads us?
To others, that could make us hard to fathom—
not wholly knowable. Even to ourselves.

THINGS THEY LEFT BEHIND

Grandmother's ration book from World War II.
Grandfather's gavel from the meetings he chaired.
Somebody's nurse's cape, silky, Navy blue.
Yellowing Gazette announcing WAR has been declared.

Christmas cards kept for ages, senders long dead.
Going back a century, a few silver dollars.
Toys whittled out of wood. Soldiers made of lead.
Full-skirted bathing suits. Gutta-percha collars.

Albums of preserved flowers, nurtured to be wilted.
Antimacassars and embroidered tablecloths.
Bundles of the quilt squares that never got quilted.
Woolen wraps that reek of things unsavory to moths.

Father's cigarette case, art deco, dented.
Mother's wedding china, only two cups broken.
A brass flask, doorknob-shaped, gun-oil scented.
Cruise liner menus, creased. One subway token.

Decommissioned, marking time, these survivors somehow
benumb us with inertia. (Well, yes, a few are nice …)
With an air of way back when, they molder on into now—
simply dying, see, to clutter up life at least twice.

MY MOTHER'S HUNDREDTH BIRTHDAY

(February 13, 2020)

Although it now is nearing seven years
since she settled back in her chair and dozed
away for the last time, her missed centennial
seems to demand some kind of taking stock.
My feelings tend to jostle with my thoughts,

shading description as it shuttles through
impassive facts and stabs of sympathy.
She was gently reared in Philadelphia,
the sheltered daughter of a minister.
Her bad-luck birthday (Friday the 13th!)
was something bound to make her brothers tease her
until that wasn't funny anymore.
I've never seen her framed as a statistic,
though some points seem to fit a period profile:
a '20s childhood, then Depression teens,
then art school, and in wartime the one time
she earned a salary (a meager one,
matching ink colors for Curtis Publishing—
the kind of work computers now make light of).

... Marriage, children, submersion in the postwar
mid-century middleclass dream of Levittown.
At last the move to the yearned-for bigger "place"
she and our father had some happy years in
but went on too long nesting in together
while his health ebbed and he became less able
to hold a job but would have rather died
than have her go to work to pay the bills.
What went wrong was a tangled interplay
of things within and outside their control:
on the one hand, his ever-lengthening list
of illnesses, but on the other, her
wholesale agreement that the only work
that suited her was doling out his pills.
Nothing could jar their mutual defense pact,
a mix of love, defiance, and helplessness.
By the time he died her care of him
almost curatorial, had become
a homemade substitute for a career.

The story possibly would seem less plaintive

if she had kept on painting. Canvases,
almost all from art school, filled her walls,
accumulating age along with her.
All of them skillful, some of them beautiful.
A few figures (omitting one or two nudes
that stayed propped and sheeted in the attic),
but mostly flowers posed in tasteful vases.
I don't believe that it was indolence
that held her back from trying other subjects.
It was a streak of grim perfectionism
that nagged at her the way she nagged at me
to make my homework, right or wrong, *look neater*.
She couldn't face the prospect of her best
brushwork falling short of mirroring
the subtler tricks of light her eyes took in.
Small differences in shades fixated her.
When women spoke to her in admiration
of her wavy, black-as-midnight hair,
she would correct them deferentially,
explaining it was really "chestnut brown."
She put aside her paints and in her gardens
set out colors that grew up from the dirt
gratefully, happily, and didn't snub her.
Rock gardening was her favorite: tiny stars
or pinwheels spanning the spectrum, thrusting up
from pockets of coarse soil: she made it happen.

After our father's death it wasn't long
before dementia brought out all the anger
she had suppressed for decades, and this was,
as she in her more lucid moments realized,
no fun for anyone. But this too passed.
After a rocky transfer to the nursing home
she became less combative, then content.
Visiting, we might find her peacefully
absorbed in exercising eye and hand.

On pages of an adult coloring book
printed with thick black outlines of the flowers
she'd painted once, then planted, she filled in
each open space with aptly chosen crayon.
Of all the patients doing this "activity,"
she was the one who colored true to life;
she was the one who stayed within the lines.

And now? Although I wouldn't wish to reach
my own centennial, or come as close
to one as she did, on this day I find
the birthday gift is mine from her, a sense
that given time (it seems to work this way)
good memories crowd out bad ones, blessedly.
I still can feel the coolness of her hand
feeling my forehead when I had the measles.

AROUND THE BLOCK

Why must I always be the first to show
my face at any meeting, party, dinner?
Tired of being everyone's precursor,
I park a good way down the street from where
this evening's hosts are no doubt occupied
with pulling plates and bottles out of cupboards,
or mounding salted nuts in little bowls,
or any of the chores they'd rather not
be tied up in just when I ring the doorbell.
It's a big enough block to stroll around
in order to arrive on time, not early.
As I pace round one corner, then a second,

the slowly gentrifying neighborhood
reminds me of the one my first few years
were spent in, although that one, unlike this,
was headed down, not up, and none too slowly.
There are the same Victorian mansard houses,
some better kept than others, and the same
postage-stamp yards with sparse platoons of grass
and stoic trees, new leaves dusty already.
No one is out: they must be at their tables.

Now that I've turned the corner I must look
over my shoulder to see the sunset deepen,
pink tensing to an operatic orange,
courtesy, perhaps, of some pollution.
Even with that gigantic flare behind me,
my body throws no shadow I can see ...
This is one of those times I feel that time
is growing porous, this place now providing
a serviceable replica of my
pre-kindergarten *mise-en-scène* ... where am I?
A sound comes from a house I'm just approaching—
a stubborn window grudging its way up—
and there, framed in that upstairs corner lookout,
an older woman peers impassively,
gaze fixed not on me but on the sunset.
My grandmother used to sit like that each evening,
giving the sinking sun appreciation
for a few quiet moments, staying sometimes
until the twilight overtook the sky.

Just as I tell myself I shouldn't stare,
the woman introduces a false note
by lifting to her lips a cigarette.
Grandma never, ever smoked, of course.
(She made me promise: if I ever smoked,
I wouldn't smoke in bed. I gave my word.)

Eyes turned to the sidewalk, I pick up
my pace as sentences in counterpoint
scratch out a pointless rut of inner protest:
This isn't all that *much like Philadelphia.*
The trees there stood taller, and the street
had to be wider (room for the trolley rails).
It would be warmer there this time of year.
And the air had its own damp rusty smell …

I thought I'd come too early, but it feels
as though I've come too late. I check my watch.
Another corner, one more after that
and I should be where I should be on time.
And sunset maybe will have burnt itself out.

A MANTEL CLOCK

The clock runs fast. Each weekly winding
comes face to face with that same finding.
Can it outpace time? Should I let it?
No, I decide. I must reset it.
So: I compel the pendulum
to take a breather, dangling plumb.
I let some moments pass, then wind
once hands are bound to be behind.
I know the thing will now read slow
for a few days. I also know
how soon the unrelenting tick,
just as unchastened, just as quick,
will not just catch up but exceed

what I would rather be its speed.

This weekly (maybe weakly) chore
(this simpleminded tug-of-war)
seems to come sooner each time round.
The chime takes on a gibing sound.
And rightly so, I'm forced to say,
as, synchronized, day follows day.
No fingers tinkering with the dial
can hold time back the slightest while.
Even told right, time runs too fast.
Racing it, I will come in last.

AFTER THE FACT

Of course by now I've been through this before:
hearing out of the blue that an old friend
has died, and not even all that recently.
Hearing this not as news but just in passing,
a thing that everyone's supposed to know,
a casual aside that manages
to throw my sense of things clear out of balance.

I would feel sad in any case, but what
I want to understand is why my sorrow,
late in arriving, seems to strike more deeply.
Surely it's laced with anger—at myself,
for being out of touch and, with less justice,
at those who knew and didn't tell me sooner.
Chagrin—that what to me is undiluted
shock, to others counts as incidental.

And souring all, absurd embarrassment
for having been a comfortable dupe,
for having all this while held for granted
a presence that had turned into an absence.

It's easy to be philosophical
gazing at stars, knowing that some we see
are orphaned glints of fires long since burnt out.
But this brings dark and distance close to home,
knowing my life for some time now has been
part of his afterlife. Confounding gaps
in time and space between the stars cast awe,
and so in this unsparing way does this
out-of-date update, just now filling a gap
in my knowledge, tearing one open in my life.

FOR GARY ENTSMINGER

Gary, I've been thinking of all the birds
you welcomed to your feeders
or tracked in swoops and darts across a page
to set before your readers:

ravens, pelicans, vireos, yes, and more
you conjured out of Colorado sky,
or veering back, Virginia's softer blue.
Their suddenness, the way they caught your eye

is ours to keep, now you yourself have flown,
sudden as plumage flashing out of sight.
Outside my window now, a twilight song

is calling home late foragers for the night.

Poet and bird—why not say birds of a feather?
Each in his way brings heaven and earth together.

LEONARDO'S VITRUVIAN MAN

When he was trying out, or breaking in
the latest pen or metal-pointed stylus,
Leonardo's habit was to write
Tell me in the margin of a notebook.
He used his finest point in drawing this
imposing nude who turns up on the cover
of many a textbook on the Renaissance.
Standing within a square that overlaps
a circle, but is mostly framed within it,
with his four arms and four legs fully stretched
to reach the boundaries of both square and circle,
he's bound to look, as Huckleberry Finn
remarked about another figure drawing,
a little "spidery." The doubled limbs,
which might have made a lesser limner fumble,
were no hard lift for this one. Either pair
of legs, straight or spread-eagled, either pair
of arms, right-angled from his trunk or upraised,
is perfect in its ratio to the rest,
proportion being what it's all about.
His navel (unlike Adam, he does have one)
marks the exact center of the circle,
his genitals the center of the square.
A naked man tailored to his environs,

a man of perfect mold, encompassed by
ruler-and-compass lines that do not lie—
and this, we understand, is meant to be
a glyph of human-cosmic harmony.

The square is grounded while the circle seems
poised to ascend like a hot air balloon
while never managing to elude the touch
of the man's feet and fingertips—a touch
which feels its limit but which cannot grasp it.
There are some things beyond our own reach here.
Is this an image, say, of aspiration?
Or tantalization? Is Vitruvian Man
master or captive of geometry?

The outspread muscles' fine, incisive lines
are confidently governed by the artist's
occasional forays at dissecting corpses,
as dexterous, one imagines, with a blade
as with the metal point he used to draw this.
Just one more facet of a lifelong, ardent
unleashing of his curiosity,
piercing the borderlines of art and science.

Speaking of curiosity, why is it
so little has been said about the face
of this protagonist who, one might think,
should prize the perfect fit of his surroundings?
Look for a smile of dominance or triumph,
and what you find is manifest ill temper
glaring from under an unruly mane.
He looks, in fact, like Thomas Jefferson
having a bad day. Almost as if
his eyes fixing on ours divine our question:
This hinge of history that haunts a gazer,
this mighty stab at putting Man (any man)

at the center of this bleeding world of ours—
how well has that been working out for us
throughout five centuries and counting? Tell me.

MUSCLE MAN

The child wasn't scared of skeletons.
They looked easy to kick apart; they had
nothing to see or smell with; they could only
go on grinning with their silly teeth.
But on a nearby page of his big children's
gateway book designed for future doctors,
there was a character that proved disturbing
enough to give him nightmares now and then.
"Muscle Man" he called it, sensibly:
a vivid anatomical illustration
of a man with skin removed to show
all of his muscles as they clung to one
of those unscary skeletons and made it
a form to flinch at.

                For intent observers,
there comes a point at which monstrosity,
without giving up strangeness, grows familiar.
Poring over the image periodically,
the boy could not have said when, in his mind,
the thing got dignified by pronoun slippage—
quite soon, though "he " had muscled "it" aside.
And this made Muscle Man, if anything,
even more creepy. Everything about him
repelled: the muscles' bulgings and striations,

their swathing of the shape like some organic
mummy wraps, or (was it?) rubber bands,
gathered in sheaves, stretched taut from head to toe.
The color was a kind of grayish-pink
(the boy would think disgustedly of earthworms).
Unlike a skeleton's, this hairless head
had two eyes looking out of it. At *him*.
No one could look more naked (after all,
somewhere, out of the picture, thankfully,
all three layers of skin had been shucked off).
Some smaller pictures in the margins showed him
using himself—swinging a sledge hammer,
plying a shovel, bending a bow. He looked
like someone sent from an unfriendly planet,
engaged in staging gruesome parodies.

Who'd want to meet him? The boy felt relief
each time he closed the book on him, and each
time he opened it he felt a sense
of clamminess when coming to that page.
His visits to the image petered out
once he moved on to books with denser text
and pictures that were plainly not totemic.

For reasons well beyond his fixed aversion,
he became something different from a doctor
when he grew up. As just another patient,
over the years he put out of his mind
the flayed, intimidating bogy-figure
until he tore first one, and then his other
rotator cuff, and couldn't lift his arms
above his shoulders without stifling
a yell that just as well could be a curse.
Talk about the return of the repressed …
Muscle Man wasn't any more appealing
to him in retrospect, but he could see

that any muscles that might give him grief
were no one's but his own, so long neglected,
paying back insults now beneath his skin.

THE RESTIVE RETIREE

Well fixed, done with the daily grind:
we'd like to envy him, but find
a cone of negativity
surrounds this recent retiree.
When he tramps out to take a walk
he nods, but doesn't stop to talk.
Neighborhood kids have learned to stay
well out of his disgruntled way.

Sentenced to life bereft of any
need to earn an honest penny,
after his decades fending stress
he's not at ease with easiness.
Once the weekend brightly beaconed.
Now a weekend's charms are weakened.
Duties rescinded can't be shirked.
Days off, quick breathers while he worked,
tick along ruthless in extension.
Month after month sucks up his pension.
Many have chimed in to suggest
he needs a hobby or a quest.
(Asking them, though, what that should be
dampens their volubility.)

Sitting, he fidgets; stands and paces.

Pleasure is void in this oasis.
What's to be done with him? His look
is blank as his appointment book,
when he's not actively irate
comparing his inactive state
to undertakings left behind
that once could occupy his mind
enough to crowd out care, and keep
him busy till he welcomed sleep.

It's not so much he loved to be
at work. It was identity.
When he looks fit to kick the cat,
nothing is what he's angry at:
no forms that need his signature,
no day's receipts to keep secure,
no deals to seal, no decks to swab—
nothing to do that does the job.

POSTAL PIECES

Stationery

How facilely the last of any band,
whether it's a Mohican or an ocher
maple leaf losing its grip on a twig,
taps a vein of spurious poignancy.
Although the only thing remarkable
in such outliers is their being extant,
they nudge us into sympathy: absurd.
Or so I say, annoyed to find myself

detained by a blank sheet of letter paper
carpeting a pasteboard box's bottom,
orphaned without a matching envelope.
Meant to be sent but clearly going nowhere,
it meets my eyes with its own eyeless gape.
Something is rivetingly cheerless here.
Ivory, deckle-edged, a bit austere,
it might have hosted a condolence note.
But now? It looks more like the cause of one:
impassively exhibiting its pallor,
laid out stationary in a box.

*

Envelopes

Idle when empty, when replete
they lend themselves to wanderlust,
shunting the freight that you entrust
from state to state, from street to street.

Keeping your tidings under wraps
until the designated slot
allows them entry—is there not
a quester's triumph here? Perhaps.

To send one trekking on its way,
unless you're partial to self-stick,
you need to give the flap a lick.
A smidgen of your DNA

rides shotgun with each billet-doux
(or with each check that pays a bill).
Not many think about this. Still,
to chauffeur round some bits of you

is something these do tidily.
You trust them, meanwhile, to confide
whatever else you placed inside
to no one but the addressee.

Addressed to him, addressed to her,
those lines might complicate a life.
Small wonder if a handy knife
should disembowel the messenger.

LATER LIFE

(Apologies to Charlotte Brontë)

We used to think it hard for the Rochesters
(I mean, for him and the second Mrs. R.),
crammed into that cottage just downhill
from the charred, tumbled ruins of the Hall.
Alone at first, and finding his way back
into life with his scars and damaged sight,
he was eerie to come upon at dusk,
weaving through ground mist with a short-leashed dog
who knew when it was time to turn toward home.
To us, his longtime neighbors, he just seemed
outmoded and pathetic, a provincial
Lord Byron with bad eyes instead of clubfoot,
but still the haughty swing of cape and cane.
Out in the morning, casting a long shadow,
he frightened children with his glassy stare;

once out of earshot, though, they let out giggles.

This was during the first weeks after the fire.
(Nobody talked of how *that* came about.)
Then, just as we were getting used to sightings
of him stumping past as in some allegory
of hubris earning its deserved reproof,
she came back and made the picture stranger.
Here, in a quiet, spread-out place like this,
things come about that often can surprise us.
Before we took it in quite, they were married,
and after a conventional interval
the former governess brought forth an heir.

So, finally, evening walks displayed all three:
she and he, arm-in-arm, the little boy,
once he had grown enough to be included,
straying behind them, bored and kicking pebbles.
She had a way of guiding the repentant
rakehell that made him feel he was in charge.
(Still something of the governess when it served her.)
Later, all of them home before full dark,
passersby could glimpse her through a window,
writing, writing in a lamp's rosy glow.
Could it be letters to that missionary
one-time suitor, still devoted friend,
gone to bring Gospel light to India?
We wondered. Then, of course, the book came out.
Sensation! And a monstrous deal of money.
They could have gone away to any place
they fancied after that, and yet they stayed.

And she grew, in a modest way, more regal.
Now, when they walk past, people seeing her
neatly turned out, chin tilted, snugly bonneted,
bestowing gracious nods or murmured greetings,

sense a resemblance to the present Queen.
Beside her, his flamboyance seems to dim,
his stride curtailed to match her shorter steps.
And she? Her tired writing wrist relaxes
by resting on his crook'd alpaca sleeve.
Which of these two is now the Personage?
Why should they care? They've come to like the cottage;
they've had their version of the way it happened
put into print for all the world to gasp at,
and gasp it has. And does. How to sum up?
Reader, she married him. He became her subject.

LIBRARY GNOMES

I. *Then and Now: The Catalogue*

Vital statistics from all seven floors,
once cramped on cards in now-discarded drawers,
exalted to the Cloud, abide unseen
till odic clicks divulge them on a screen.

II. *Not for Circulation*

Think of the monks who kept their volumes chained,
prizing the lessons vellum leaves contained,
with value added for the pains it took
each hand that slaved for months to pen each book.

III. *Classical Philosophy Section*

Telling us how to live: they had a nerve!
Their maxims landed like attacks on us.
Soberly bound, unthumbed, these tomes preserve
their spurned advice. They've turned their backs on us.

IV. *Reading Room*

A fidgeter provokes his chair to creak.
A colleague paces round in shoes that squeak.
A student snores. Three others carry on,
rehashing dates best not to tarry on.
Their whispers would be right at home on stages.
No sound arises, though, from turning pages.
Asking for silence would be special pleading:
it seems that I'm the only one here reading.

V. *If Only*

Had Alexandria's scrolls been digitized,
we could read Sappho's lines without those gaps.
We'd have her lyrics' fire as first devised,
not fragments coldly gleaned from mummy wraps.

VI. *Date Stamp*

This book, last taken out in '83,
is more than ready to be held by me.

Riffling pages, I can hear a sigh:
it's waited all these years, and now is why.

VII. *Inside Out*

Suppose our bodies were inside our minds.
We'd be enveloped by ethereal rinds.
And having only thoughts on which to feed,
we just might choose more wisely things to read.

THE TETRAGRAMMATON

Appraising the Creation's artistry,
our connoisseurship dithered in the dark
for too long, searching for the Maker's mark.
Where, and upon what medium, would it be,

the self-attributing, the taking credit?
Could it be scored grand on a canyon wall,
or etched on one mere snowflake? Great or small,
we could not rest until we'd found and read it;

surely an artist signs his masterpiece.
The world's great gallery flung each dimension
open to us, indulging our attention
patiently, as we ransacked without cease …

Until, on some unlovely crowded street,
wearied, we met the long-sought signature

glinting from grooves in faces of the poor,
shearing from us each previous conceit.

We blinked then, smitten by that flash of light:
Your **h**oly name **w**as **h**idden in plain sight.

TEACHING POETRY

Today we teach the poem: trace the way
images flicker and cohere and cluster,
remark how rhymes give point to what lines say,
how words themselves take on a tender luster
when they are chosen with uncommon sense
by someone whose five senses are aligned
keenly to catch Creation's radiance
and draw it dazzling through a reader's mind.

We sift through style in a search for meaning.
For all we find, some final clue lies hid.
Rooting deep in us, though, to grow up greening,
the poet's words restyle our lives amid
renewed awareness of what's obvious:
We do not teach the poem. It teaches us.

POSTSCRIPT AHEAD OF TIME

Pages mount up. How many more
will host my cursive jots before
writing and I have reached an end?
Here, for the record, I'll append
lines to round out the final sheet
of any text left incomplete.
I searched for words. They came and found me,
sprang up like seedlings all around me.
Beckoned by them, I wandered through
their branching ways. With them I grew.
For that, they have my full-grown thanks.
And once I'm plucked from mortal ranks
I'll trust them still to speak for me
with mottled singularity.
Let them give homage to the Word
by whom the leaves of life are stirred.
What I write now, let them say then.
And let the last word be Amen.

From *Comforting the Wilderness* (1977)

For Robert Fitzgerald

BOSTON SUNDAY DINNER

More grandly than a camel kneeling down
in desert twilight she assumed her place,
motioning me to join her at her right.
Spooky, I thought, this dining in state for two,
at one corner of a table built for twelve.
Her hand lay on the table like pressed wax,
the bones too easily seen, but beautiful.
A prism hung to the cord of a window blind
sprinkled a bracelet of rainbow on her wrist.
December; and the light was dropping off early,
but even in winter dusk her silver showed
the chastened glow of a century's polishing.
I puzzled over the function of my forks,
abashed by the graying, apron-clad retainer
shuffling toward me with a plate of soup.
The last remaining help, unused to company.
Most of the talk has left me. Only a few
sentences I remember, each one prefaced
by an apologetic almost-cough.
"Literary men now are no longer what
they were in my day, in my father's day.
My father used to see James Russell Lowell
walking on Brattle Street in his English suits.
You know that he was our Ambassador.
I don't suppose we've had a poet since
presentable enough for such an office.
Well, poets may be better unpresentable. ..."
I mused over the room we just had left
and would return to: utterly insufficient
fireplace, sooty portraits, sets of Scott
and Trollope, obvious volumes read to pieces.
Fur of her three cats tufted the furniture. ...
I made my answers while the rainbow band

retreated down the table from us, flashed
at last on the far paneling; when I looked
again, was gone entirely. Shadow filled
the air like a fine ash; suddenly even she
began to feel it. So she called out, "Emily!
"If you please! The lights!" (No guest of hers
rose from her table to approach a light switch.)
Again the gray lady entered, touched the wall,
illumining us, and turned to take our dishes.
I saw their faces side by side for an instant
under the good light. Sisters they might have been.

GARGOYLE

An ornamental bung,
a dragon-dog in little,
a throat without a tongue
to sample its own spittle:

whatever I may be,
harpy or horned toad,
is all the same to me.
I labor to erode.

Good Christians, as you go
about your wonted kneeling,
be thankful you're below
a serviceable ceiling.

For centuries I've craned
my neck above your city

and never yet complained.
I am above your pity.

And you are under mine.
I dream: a day will come
of which I am the sign.
Smitten grotesquely dumb,

you'll glare to see each other sprout
tusk, antler, serrate tail,
and the appalling snout.
I trust fate not to fail,

when even today on just
and unjust Heaven can strew
that soot-laden rain I must
catch, convey, and spew.

JACK-O'-LANTERN

Candle, spoon and carving knife:
nearing the vigil of the dead,
let's impose a little life
upon a ripening, faceless head.

Slice and pry the handled top,
shovel out the mush and seeds,
cut—before we hear the clop,
coming too close, of phantom steeds.

Two triangles make the eyes,

another makes a classic nose;
three teeth, square and oversize,
complete a countenance that glows

all night by its captive wick,
its parody of intellect.
Idle amusement for the quick.
And yet the venturous dead are checked:

shades of traitors that are given
one night's leave of Satan's jaws;
throngs of warlocks, wild unshriven
things with lammergeyer claws;

bogies by the wide heavens abhorred
witness their own defective will
when they see this grinning gourd
presiding on our window sill.

Of whom or what an effigy,
that is for itself to know
until All Hallows' turn us free
to lift the cranial lid and blow.

A STUDY

Hung to the ceiling's centerpoint, he seems
to accent every other vertical.
This is the way a room grows tall in dreams,
escaping up beyond human recall.
Too much is here to take in at once, and we

hunt with our eyes for something familiar to hold to.
Twilight eddies in corners, almost blue.
Afternoon dust alights on the motionless globe.
There where he laid it aside the study key
glints at a grazing touch of departing sun.
Here the feeling is one of work routinely done,
of wastebaskets put to use with seemly frequency.
Docketed, paid bills, uncluttered blotters testify
to an archaic, resolute but affable efficiency.

That was it: having made his effects as neat
as might befit a man of considered action,
he set himself to perform this final feat
of incredible abstraction.
Drawn by his weight the ceiling creaks.
Hairline cracks begin to radiate
outward from the firm hook that held the chandelier.
Discouraging inquiry, he sets the dominant line
toward any who would seek for entrance here.
For see, around his axis gravitate
such bevies of objects now bereft of care:
pipe racks and pens and the heads of state, signed,
serve only to frame a dangled figure and await
the paced evaporation of his tension.
And we, his audience, who forced the door
open to see him, see him in just this state
and gather to a quiet minute's halt here before
a willing suspension.

FROM ASHES

Sometimes a man comes home to find his house
burnt to the floor and no fire left to fight.
Stray sparks glint between splinters of glass.
No one is home and no home stands and it is a cold night.

And the scene is deep in trees. And no moon shows.
Trees never caught and they keep him there in the dark.
Pine trees sifting the wind bend and brush elbows,
differing whether he'll bother setting to work

to set to rights the black hulks of his beams
leaning unevenly over his late concerns—
the ashy pulp of papers and books whose names
are hard now to remember. Now he learns

to notice the basic, charred bones of the house,
bent pipes, fused wires, a battered sink—
boring necessities made precious by loss.
Hearing the gossipy pines, he tries to think:

Was it lightning? Did the cat chew on a wire?
Did the wind help? Why didn't he live in town,
where neighbors are near and trees are tame and fire
attracts attention? Nobody's house burns down

nowadays. All his woes are out of style,
like his address. Who else happens to be
deprived of a big red hook-and-ladder while
flames eat up his shingles? He can see

only so far: Privacy didn't pay.
His one pet lies minus her nine lives.
Now what? Walk off and leave it, the way

men will abandon bad cars or their wives?

O ashes will all be cold by morning, morning,
mutter the pines, his proxy family, till he
turns on his heel, hard. But he hears a ping
down by his foot: this is that extra key

scuffed from under what was a doormat. When
he holds it in his hand his trees become
silent, as if suddenly seared. A man
clings to his title. Sometimes a man comes home.

SNAKE CROSSING

Bullet headed, horsewhip tailed,
soundless, side-winding, nattily scaled,
it is a wonder anything fully solid
should flow so vividly quick through every part.
It swipes from thicket into opposing thicket.
Marking an end to one day's wanderlust,
I stand in the crossed path with joints made gelid,
hoping to slow my jumpiness of heart,
eyeing the faint, linked esses in the dust,
a sketchy hiss that I spell out in silence.

IN WITNESS

For Robert Fitzgerald

My way lay through a wood.
Under a guise of trees
all my old familiars stood,
off limits by law.
I recognized the species
of every one I saw,

even despite the lack
of leaves on all that lumber.
Now that I was back
I dropped my old esteem
and sought amid their number
a remnant to redeem.

I snapped a twig or two
to make a test,
and saw the blood flow
from the wormy bark.
I wandered west,
trailed after by the dark.

Gathering branches here and there
I could dream that I was led
by the Harrower
of the waste, wild land
who went harvesting the dead
with no hook but a hand.

One twig was sound and green.
That one I would keep.

I came to a clearing then,
round, empty and as good
as any place to sleep.
There I dropped my dead wood

and kindled it to fire
the better to banish fear.
But as the flames grew higher
my single green twig cried,
"Lord, if you had been here
my brothers had not died."

THE PAUSE

Only a slow-growing forest, met with
in the warming cleft of summer,
would have hosted such a moment—
that is where we were.

No living owner's name
was posted where we came to earth.
Slivered seed-hulls, winter litter
lay round like brown manna,

in the oval clearing abandoned
cones dried and raveled to tinder.
Nearby a forking stream
swam over tracts of pebbles, they

were creviced and gray as pebbles
dug from the dark side of the moon.

How shall I say what happened?
Summer came to a standstill,

birds grew sober, limp air mingled
into the crowns of trees and put away
puffing, maybe for good.
The stream ran sudden as blood

but it was all that ran.
Even our fates stood off awhile,
tireless, but disengaged,
broadly considering us the way

we might look at children tranced in play.
Cool eyes fanned over us like leaf-shadows.
Halfway up the pines sunlight
may have played, for all I know,

in needles, priming the points, but
by then our eyes were shut.

GRASS WIDOWS

Your dandelions dotting half
a casual summer lawn
mature to let their fertile chaff
uncouple and be gone;

a chance breeze or a child's puff
yellow-buttons leagues of green.
Call it a Life Force? Call it fluff.

The tatty clusters mean

whatever you may wish them to,
breathing abroad the seed
that's found a go-between in you.
Insouciantly weed,

these have neither toiled nor spun:
like their lily neighbor
lean at ease in rain or sun,
blest for lack of labor.

And labor's lost. Grass grows unmown.
You watch them grow up gold
and thick as midnight stars were shown
to Abraham, grown old.

ANOTHER DAY

That morning tide, that upswing of the air,
wages against the wing of the house I lie in;
tuning now to its waves, my curtain rings
clink like a bustling housekeeper's bunch of keys.
Sleepers, awake: for doors and stairs are creaking musically,
skirling as though the entire house
were stretching in the sun,
letting the dew steam off its chalky shingles.
Linen quivers; a warm barny smell
rides in at the window. Light is taking sway:

the firmament of shadow overhead

sifts out of the room, revealing
unmysterious ceiling. Square and white,
its four corners boast no dangling spies.
Once again I dreamt of dead relations,
Grandmother in the garden, another summer,
pinching a done flower from its stem,
yesterday's day-lily.
Handing it to me absently, passing on
—into what hidden place? No protocol
governs these wordless meetings.

So often now I'm strange to my own skin.
I could be standing there at the door—
not now, but twenty years from now—
taking this in, from the sun's first
foothold, a thin, quaking beam
where pinhead seraphs conjured out of dust
exult and swarm. And see, my heavier
self lies long and motionless in bed,
grown a sounder sleeper, guessing nothing at all,
till the light widens, and the wind
blows the white curtains in.

From *The Wonder of Seeing Double* (1988)

For Catherine and Tony

NARCISSUS

This match was made in heaven, or let's say
confected in a patch of fallen sky
idling under your avid contemplation,
hot young hunter here pinned to the brink
of waters you once hunkered down to drink.
How long ago was that? There's no before,
no after, all's a privileged moment snared
in cool solution, not precipitating
even beneath your gripped and melting gaze.
Here is the end. The end will be to see
all and yet never enough in one pale face
looking helplessly up as you lean down
and the woods drift from gray to green to brown.
Never to heed or hasten or grow old,
no eye for the new leaf timidly unfolding,
nor for the sun that broadly winks in passing
over your acne-pitted shoulder at
the object floating unattained and chaste
as that sweet medium for ever holding
still, as still as it can, for your slow take.
No echo sounds. How can the hunt be over?
The dream will not be told until you wake.
What would it take, a magic word to free you,
letting the figure loose to join the flow?
All you can do is let the lover see you,
having long ceased to listen, speak, or know.

ECHO

You here again? Of course, I should have known:
spring outshouted you with a chortle of
nest builders and nonce rivulets, cheering the sun,
summer covered your calls in vibrant green.
Now when bewildered trunks, crown-scattered, stand
ranked in chorus ordered to be resonant
of loss long to be borne, you sound among them:
Here! and again Here! But where is Here?
Before, behind, the winter-hollowed woods
offer you alcoves as I lean and listen,
wondering what first sent you wandering, sad
Effect for ever yearning to meet and mate
with callous Cause, likely not worth your while.
In the pause after the period your poor would-be
rejoinder hangs in the breathing space, more inquiry
than answer, ever aggrieved to hang unanswered.
Further words, while the voice holds, defer
your making known your wavering whereabouts;
but silences entice you nearer home,
as I have come to know in shortening days
hard by a brook gone mum with ice, my ear
locating you at last so close you might
after all be huddled in its crimped labyrinth,
murmuring Here, as I hear and again hear you.

FAMILY ALBUM

Some fiddling with the lens,
some flattery with the light—
and Smile! We smile. Snap!
Our smiles, deft as wrens,
clearing the shutter flap,
take roost within the little box of night.

Latent on celluloid,
our likenesses await
favorable developments:
unviewed, their spell is void.
Must we amass evidence—
hems or hair, wedding rings we can date—

that things aren't as they were?
Evidently we must.
Jarring our own focus, Time's
remodelings make a blur,
scenes of his petty crimes
fast fading but for curatorial lust

to clutch at what we know
did not, could never last.
Embalmed in silver salts,
our former selves are slow
to anger, blind to faults,
look up with hope, forgiving all that's past.

"Look, I was thinner then."
"That must have been the year
they cut the maple down."
"Which one of her young men
was that?" "Just some poor clown."

"There's the old tractor Uncle let you steer." …

Snap the book shut. Our seeing
will never match the flash
that riveted these frail,
fluttering plumes of being.
Blinking aside detail,
the eye that masters tear and lid and lash

mimes rather that machine
(the Brownie's graver kin)
that scorns the surface clay
as did the shrouded Dean,
loosing a cold, lightless ray
to probe the pile of chalk that waits within.

BRIGHT ENOUGH TO SEE YOUR FACE IN

Twice a year she polished "the old silver."
This was a ceremony that demanded
towels spread out at one end of the table,
basins of soapy water and clear water,
many soft cloths, the squat jar of polish,
and, lined up for exacting treatment, things
we lived with day by day and never looked at:
the teapot hardly any company
was grand enough to merit, napkin rings
(only two: the children's were just wood),
the little tray *her* grandmother had used
for calling cards, which some unthinking piety

kept sitting unemployed in the front hall,
a child's mug which was, at least, employed
(used to hold toothpicks),—and the family spoons
brought from the rack that held two rows of ten.
(An upper row of ten, a bottom row
of nine, after a genteel kleptomaniac,
late of the Altar Guild, had made her move.)

Peering at each piece critically, she washed
and rinsed and dried it, then swabbed polish on.
It was a pink paste, and I used to think
the smell of it was pink—whatever that meant.
It wasn't pink for long; a little rubbing
made it the color of February slush
as it took every smudge unto itself.
Household magic! From a final flourish
issued a buffed-to-dazzling retinue,
ready to be set back on shelves, the spoons
hung by their bowls again to dangle proudly
handles crammed with curlicued initials.
Too good to use, they'd hang there good for nothing
but to amaze us six months further on
by how distinctly dingy they'd become,
taking on a gradual dusk of tarnish
by tinges too insidious to be noticed
till it was time to bring them down again.

She fought it back so many years, the stealthy
challenge of shadow, steady-paced corrosion
hovering in the very air we breathed.
How long is it since nineteen ovals winked
in idle brilliance at the plunging sun?
The bright idea I had of writing this
itself turns darker at the thought of time,
wearily searching for the single spoon
no pointed hints could ever conjure back

to join its showy fellows on the rack.
And where's the rack? What niece or nephew has it?
Two or three spoons that ended up with me
lie in some dresser somewhere, out of sight.
"If it's worth doing, it's worth doing right,"
she'd say, every six months, when she was done.
It isn't worth it, though, to everyone.
Sooner or later everyone gets robbed.

TO THE CRICKET

Seducer, can your song
persist, keyed-up and long
as this unsleeping night?
The notion that it might,
that a spondaic chirr
is all that might occur
until the daylight rouses
birds in their penthouses—
the thought alone would keep
the mind astray from sleep.

Outdoors, but all too near
to an unwilling ear,
the friction of your knees
breeds importunities.
Please please meet me—your cry
wheedles each passerby
to be a pampered guest
in a snug ivy nest.
For ever pitched the same,

you are immune to shame,
and never chirp the less
for nightlong unsuccess.

Is it the cleaner choice
not to give need a voice?
Your silent auditor
finds second thoughts a bore,
yet fields them even while
framing a chilly smile,
counting the hours gone
and yet to go till dawn,
glad to the point of fear
that none will ever hear
his wants—unweakening, vain—
confessed to counterpane.

EXTENDED RUN

Across the road a ragged stand of trees
putting out summer growth puts out of view
the mountain close behind.
Too warm to worry at obscurities,
as long as summer flourishes we find
the proverb proving true:
without a qualm we put it out of mind.

Only when late October turns to later,
herding the leaves determinedly away,
will it preempt the scene
like an omniscient, meddlesome narrator

blundering on to hog the stage between
the high points of the play,
telling us what we're meant to think they mean.

It was impressive, seen the first time round:
barefaced, baldpated, raked by livid scars
(inactive ski runs, those).
Under a paling sky, on chilling ground
we saw sustained this minatory pose
and wondered if our stars
had something near and dismal to disclose.

But repetition blunts apocalypse.
We pondered less the second's year's unveiling.
The flinty interludes
are curtained off as winter's rigor slips;
and, knowing what the annual rote includes,
we'll face it without quailing.
It's different with our own abeyant moods.

THE SHORTCUT

A shadow scythed across the lawn.
I saw the shadow, not the bird.
So briefly come, so briskly gone
no salient traits could be inferred

except that it could use its wings
to a superlative degree,
to judge from those quick scissorings
that sliced between the sun and me.

This image cuts more ways than one,
I said to none but my machine
that labors loud beneath the sun
to shave the ground a level green.

That shadow, aimed at beckoning shade,
lanced beyond reach of burning day—
while I with mine, blade matched with blade,
hacked out a path the longer way.

CONTEMPORARY MUSIC

The neighboring wind chime we have never seen
tinkles its giveaway through shifting gaps
in our imperfect barricade of green,
teasing its audience from hammock naps.

These aleatory noises that the ear
makes, if not music of, at least a mood
no doubt say less than we are wont to hear,
their antic peals agreeably construed

as hymning summer's gentle dispensations.
When life, too long immured, moves out of doors,
this jingling ushers us to recreations
adjourned by only flower-primping chores.

Ringing its tintinnabulary changes
on all the whispered fluencies of air,
the half-a-dozen tones it rearranges,

taxing to score, might register somewhere

between a cowbell's ruminative clatter
and thinner clinks of silver-pitchered ice.
We wonder what fine-tempered bits of matter,
launched in performance randomly as dice,

are joined in this ensemble: Venice glass
dangled in sleek medallions the sun loves?
Or, from Korea, some shell-casing's brass,
by second firing made a flock of doves?

This latest thought slides glumly into place
just now, as bombers on a training run
boom out a bass line, lumbering back to Base,
their mettle advertised, their duty done.

When all in aftermath has fallen still
we wait, impatient for the pliant chime
to play at whim, or at the wind's odd will,
keeping no time except for summertime. …

And so it does—but sounds far less emphatic
after that squadron's passing tore the sky;
a brief emergence from a blare of static.
Twisting the mind's dial, can't we try

to render dominant those frequencies
where only mild-mannered tunes are played?
But signals vary; summer's touted ease
is stricken mute beneath that droning shade.

OLD BURYING GROUND

As long as men have cleared these fields of stones
this spot has been a portion set apart
for those who cleared them to inter their bones,
their names entrusted to the carver's art.

Here sanctioned graven images adorning
legends incised below their low relief
feature in turn for every era's mourning
a choice device to give a shape to grief.

The elders ordained skulls with bear-trap teeth
hovering gleefully on harpy wings;
their sons, more civilly, repose beneath
the cherub's less aggressive flutterings.

Their grandsons, still more decorous, enjoyed
an emblem classical in its reserve:
a willow with despondent boughs deployed
to frame an urn by their condoling curve.

Marking the measured ebb of holy dread
drew smiles from these prim and bulbous *putti*,
till they absconded, leaving in their stead
lachrymal limbs to do their pious duty.

Was this the destined course of intellect,
the forfeiture of faith for sentiment?
Heaven left faceless, how can we detect
what even that third generation meant,

festooning their commemorating lines
with such pathetic shaggy dogs of trees?
Trite as their trusted proverbs, these designs

planted in rows present a pallid frieze.

Did they imagine this entablature
graven with sorrow fountaining afresh
might be a means for sorrow to endure,
perpetuating tears among their flesh?

Or had their Yankee caution coldly weighed
the likelihood their latest heirs would keep
a living vigil?—Once the bill was paid,
the willow could be counted on to weep.

CHRONOMETRICS

I. *Turning Back the Clock*

    By setting back these hands
I win an extra hour of sleep tonight
and make each winter morn a shade more bright.
    Seasonable demands

    within our sphere are met,
while nothing will draw short or slow the arc
the planet orbits through an ordered dark
    whose clock but once was set.

    Between the time we make
and that which makes away with us—the sun's
cold strategy—our hot resistance runs
    through snow for summer's sake.

II. *Digital Clock*

The days are past when people might
mistake me for a mean night light,
an exit sign, a smoke alarm.
Consider, should I fail to charm:
The circle you no longer see
has been economized in me,
a billboard changing as you blink,
diminishing your need to think
of hours past or yet to come.
The dial trailed by pendulum,
the water's lapse, the shifting sands
defer to digits. Look, no hands.

III. *Grandfather*

They stood me up, a coffin in a corner.
When no one volunteered to sound a knell,
I lifted up my hand, a willing mourner,
and let my chime supply the passing bell.

Many a midnight since I've kept my vigil
seconded by the moon upon my brow,
who changes phase and face to suit his schedule.
(His grinning sickle profile's peeping now.)

Such years I've given to this undertaking
I have forgot for whom these rites are done.
That rueful wooden clack my tongue keeps making
would serve to usher onwards anyone.

IV. *Hourglass*

Belled at top and bottom, pinched at the waist,
I move this little desert I've encased
whichever way is down. Its thin descent
mounts to a dune by steady increment.
Once multitudes convened to see me perch
at preacher's hand in each conforming church,
and as he schooled this world to meet the next
I mimed his arid sifting of his text.
No sermon runs an hour now. Nor do I.
Shrunken in stature, wrested from on high,
I time a mere three minutes for your egg.
Nothing like time to take one down a peg.

V. *Clepsydra*

By steady, sedulous embezzlement
I drain the minutes only to let flee
my liquid gains whose loss I then lament
with marks left high and dry inside of me.

At bottom I'm a leaky drinking cup
whose fill, forever listing from the brim,
must tantalize dry lips to siphon up
sips to endure this rainless interim.

Drought is the fixed condition of us all,
in exile from the everlasting springs.
The used and ruthless droplets I let fall
mimic the shimmer of the tears of things.

VI. *Sundial*

Bent-headed one, can it be time to linger
    watching my gnomon trace
the daylight's path with one black, pointed finger
    while soldered to one place?

Having become a shade you will not cast
    a shadow men can see:
rove in your three dimensions while they last,
    and leave the fourth to me.

PARTIAL DRAFT

My ear, still keyed to summer, failed to label
a murmur stirred by the mild October day;
so, lured at last mid-sentence from my table
(What was the word I wanted?—It slipped away)

I turned to see how, eased of my attention,
trees turning fast had scattered half their load.
What I was hearing, mind in meek suspension,
was former foliage hurrying down the road,

a fibrous faint grating, skip, and bustle
made when the wind dispatches lemony shoals
over the asphalt. That doom-eager hustle
whispers a dry subversion to the souls

of those still indisposed to follow after,
intent to stay awaiting a later word.
A second wind: cicada-like but softer,
the sound is known this time when it is heard:

a noise more near to silence than most noises,
bordering silent moments when the pen
upon some puzzling brink or line-break poises
before pursuing its scratchy path again.

HOMEWORK

In those last years she sewed mostly by feel.
The window by her chair did little for her;
late in the day she felt the sun lowering
and went on stitching, nodding with the rhythm,
It was a finely honed accomplishment,
something she took grim pride in. It was only
threading her needle that she needed help with.
Then the boy would put his book down and try
to spirit through the niggardly steel loophole
the slenderest of ends, which in his fingers
bulged as coarse and clumsy as a hawser,
butting the aperture it aimed to pierce.
The little eye itself would seem to wink
maliciously, repelling his rude stabs.
The thread slipped through at last as if by luck,
or in derision, finding its own way.
Slowly, with practice, he got better at it,
returning sooner each time to his homework.
Sometimes he wondered: what could it be like

to watch the prodigal colors of the world
narrowing like a peacock's closing fan
until, all suns extinguished, it became
a dull swag drawing lines across the dust?
He thought of how, years younger, he had played
tourist in his own room with his eyes shut,
coming so quickly up against a bedpost
that he gave up, disgusted. Patience came later,
partly learned from the one who sat each evening
lining her steady rows of stitches up
against the dark upwelling. When he looked
up from his page at her in her dim corner,
then quickly back to it, his eyes would blur,
as if the graphs and characters he studied
had bled their precious ink to turn the busy,
columned page a sudden, solemn black.
Then he would blink, and bend to the next problem.

THERE AND BACK AGAIN

Black from the poker's soot,
the thumbprint plants a maze
on this new leaf turned over.
The tired man whose thumb
provided this exhibit,
pondering the cunning whorls,
can picture venturing in—
shouldering a way between
carboniferous canyon walls
cast in a dismal grid.
There at the shunned center

he'd end up face to face
with what? Some horned and hoofed
incumbent hot for slaughter?
Once I might have thought it.
Now I believe he'd find
only the lost child
long ago left behind,
waiting among the ash heaps
for someone with the nerve
to lead him out of there.
Half-asleep, the boy
has propped his chin on one
or another grubby fist.
He hears a step, and stiffens.
The time to go has come.
Alive to every risk, the late
but always destined escort
is foolhardy or smart enough
to trust as compass only
his own wincing memory for
the many steps they'll take, reversed,
to be outside once more.
The way out is hard.
They lose count of the blind
alleys just avoided,
charred crimps and turns.
Somewhere—they can hear it—
a whispering fire burns.
But there it is, the final gap:
beyond it, both are free
and fearless, the man standing
stunned by the sudden whiteness:
just when could it have snowed?
He drops the boy's hand to see him
run wherever he will—
no sentries. Now he wonders

why at the grimed outermost
wicket gate did no one
straddle the path, demand to see
what some would die to flourish:
proof of identity?

THE VOICE OF THE YAWN

Bodiless though I be, if you ever could track me
down to my dark impenetrable den
in which I huddle dormant between forays,
you'd stumble over me located somewhere near
the bottom and back of the brain as it tapers
into the spinal stem, the unlighted crossing
where thought and what you like to call "being thoughtful"
descend to the brutal honesty of reflex.
It's there, when the fit is on me, that I first
make my embarrassing stirrings felt,
touching off my powder train of convulsion,
by an obscure, incessant tickling
tensing your neck and tightening your jaws,
inciting, as my dark urges burn
to declare themselves, a humid, bulbous
exhalation to occupy your mouth,
demanding to be let out or swallowed;
and as your eyes narrow and mist with tears,
your cheeks flush with propriety's exertions,
you know my power and know that not to yield
will only invite the return of the repressed.
I wish that I could predict, any better than you,
just what is needed to trigger one of my tantrums;

sermons hovering round their halfway points
are a safe bet, most any reasoned discourse
in fact runs the risk of my putting in an appearance.
Reason and all its works and I are at odds;
I am not thoughtful toward you, anyone, anything.
You ought to make the best of it, throw back
your inattentively nodding head, spread lips and let
me issue forth in operatic splendor.
You might come to cherish me for my social utility,
your faithful, misshapen dwarf of a jester
whose grotesque somersaults into your waning soiree
will send the stubbornest guests in search of their coats,
end the long evening, get you to bed at last.

SAFE HARBOR

Past midnight, and much darker
than when I hit the pillow,
I heard the channel marker
appraising every billow
whose overweighted crest
collapsed with all the rest.

Its single note, dividing
the shallow from the deep,
took on the task of guiding
me out again toward sleep,
loosing the stubborn painter.
The port lights playing fainter,

it braced me past the bold

breakwater that takes the pulse
of tides in pincer hold,
a final perch for gulls.
It tolled me seaward, till
It too, becalmed, held still

and the unfathomed sea
again made room for me.

SPRING'S AWAKENING

Oddly assorted bedfellows, frost and thaw
ruckus under their scanty quilt of clay.
To them, spring comes as the final straw.
Their tortured nights are pictured plain as day
in sudden humps and craters that we find
in garden ground upheaved and undermined.

Tossing about, all elbows in the cramped
embrace to which their restless kind are fated,
their lust for loamy struggle never damped
in all the years since they were strangely mated,
neither has known the other's throes to yield
to careless calm. Their bed's a battlefield.

Curious: what they fight is what they share—
a sullen trance where serial nightmares reign.
Scouting the damage spades will soon repair,
shouldn't we be less ready to complain?
Our cruelest dreams have yet to match the girth
of these, that wrench the surface of the earth.

THE FLOATER

They always used to say, demanding elders,
schoolmasters in manner or in fact,
that this boy was a hopeless drifter, lacked
direction, drive, and didn't give a damn.
Floating face to the sky on a summer lake,
not getting anywhere fast, he called to mind
calmly the old reports of still no progress,
and knew them true—years, years had passed,
and here he was, the flagrant foil to their
frustrations which he could not make his own.
And there was no excuse. He hadn't been there
to watch his father running to catch that train,
only imagined the platform-edging gravel
galling the knees, the loaded briefcase tumbled,
the fingers popping off the collar button.
Some people can't relax to save their lives.
Arching his back on water's ample roundness,
marveling how it will just as soon uphold
a hippo or a splinter, he felt drained of weight
and curiously transparent, like a teardrop
gliding across a wide unblinking eye.

THE INVENTION OF ZERO

Arithmetic's anonymous Hindu hero
altered the sum of things by adding zero,

ushering digits upward place by place

to scout the outer curve of outer space.

Immensities of distance, mass, and weight
came to be prey and play of chalk and slate,

bane to our sophomore doodling his exam.
Can't we inspire him to a dithyramb

on powers compact within the simple o?
The world itself was made *ex nihilo*.

THEIR VOICES

I used to hear them late at night, the voices
back on Saturdays, back in that neighborhood,
down below, loudening out of the distance,
blurring away again before too long.
There was a lot of laughter, not very bright.
Now and then a few lines of a song.
I would remember words, notes, if I could,
some little souvenir of some lost night,

but nothing now survives for exact quotation.
I lay on the long dimming edge of sleep,
heard them scuffing the gritty curb of manhood.
They talked about the girls they'd been to see,
or what a motherfucker Charlie was.
Through chainlink fence, exhaust-afflicted air,
and dusty leaves of a lone ailanthus tree,
all this intelligence filtered up to me.

So much more than a couple of city
blocks, lots, and storeys stand
between us now, my nights have grown
so quiet of late with certainty.
Here in a time of so much known for sure,
I wonder how it would be to hear their voices
rising free and so soon falling away,
stupidly happy, ignorant of the choices
made for them long ago, long nights before.

ASH WEDNESDAY, LATE AFTERNOON

Dust-motes bustling up—or is it
in, or through—the afternoon's
lazily sloping chute of light
seem intent above all to scatter
havoc along the grand
avenue that irradiates
their antics, unprogressive, up *and* down,
I now see, tracking one or two
only to lose them soon in the lit swarm.
Inflamed with no mere ardor now to rise
but at whatever risk to swing and shine
in these remoter regions of the sun's decline
they do, in fact, dazzle as they conduct
carnival turns and vaults in bliss above
their stunned confederates thickening on the carpet—
the fatal plain to which they too
will settle. Don't they know it? When they do,
they will have lost their audience, hung
in cooling air, the sun's last ladder rung

tweaked from beneath them, finding this to be
an unappreciative arena where
the act winds down after the spotlight's moved.
Their ultimate stunts, in graying vacancy,
are dartings we can take only on trust,
picturing that deserted turbulence
dimly subsiding, mating dust to dust.

A TIME PIECE

For C. F. S.

Again, the daily swing.
Your flashing, clamorous arc
grows wider as you grow;
your high delighted hum
startles the sleepy park.
On from the fast-decamping snow
and puddled green of spring,
it's been our place to come.

More than a year old now,
all day you're on the run.
Later, the rocking horse
and rocking chair likewise
will certify your day as done
by cantering through their course.
The days are laced with cold now;
gold leaves excite your eyes.

At last the swing hangs plumb.
The motions of your day,
the evening's hurried blue,
sway even me toward sleep.
In earnest as in play
may I keep time with you,
the only pendulum
that gives me time to keep.

MORNING EXERCISE

For A. P. G. S.

My son assists me shaving.
On a laundry hamper lid
he sits, big-eyed, behaving,
watching the busy skid

of blade leveling stubble
his chin has yet to sprout.
An urge to be my double
is what it's all about,

and so I lend him lather
(there's plenty for us both)
to play at being father
while I cut back on growth.

I notice, bending nearer,
the decades' detriments,

then try the kindlier mirror
his upturned face presents.

Admiring how intently
he pares his suds away,
I view my flesh more gently.
Now for another day.

JUST HERE AND NOW

I couldn't give any reason for slowing down,
just here and now, bedazzled by a solitary
mailbox you could see from half a mile,
a loaf of white heat. Half the summer might go by
without its red flag ever perking up.
Coming closer now tugs into view
the ragged patch of chicory it stands in,
bent spokes of petals dusted by wheels gone by.
The fence behind is here and there missing a picket
as if a dog determined to be playful
had run off into the orchard with it.
From here a drive more dirt than gravel rises
past a barn that hasn't seen paint
in God knows how many years,
up to a turn-around where three or four cars
(it's hard to count) continue patiently
to rust in various states of disassembly.

Why have I stopped? Just possibly, because
nothing is here that is not plausible.
It's hotter by the minute.

The house can just be seen between the shade trees;
that must be the kitchen window.
Yellow curtains. Without a doubt, inside,
a spool of flypaper twirls from a ceiling light,
and doesn't ever manage to catch enough.
The floorboard cracks have long since come to be
a crucial part of the linoleum pattern.
The oven door hangs like a drawbridge down.
How could anyone bake on a day like this?
But the older daughter is just done icing a cake.
She hands her small sister
the large spoon to lick.
And nothing could be more proper:
it is the little girl's birthday.
(How do I know? I just do.)
Being nine at last has gone to her head.

Looking out the window,
she sees the blue roof of my car
and wonders when they'll take her to see the ocean.
She pops the spoon in her mouth
and sights along the handle
like Daniel Boone drawing a bead on a squirrel.
Like all of us, she loves to make more of less.
She is lost in the sweet wonder of seeing double:
two windows, two mailboxes, two
cars stopped for no reason there on the road—
until her sister, seventeen, so much taller,
tells her for it must be the twentieth time
that if she won't quit crossing her eyes they'll stick.

From *The Post Office Murals
Restored* (1994)

For my Mother and Father

SERVING THE PURPOSE

You know those shims you make by folding paper
over and over in a tightening square?
You jam one under a china cupboard's foot
to stop its rattling every time you pass.
It does the job, and you forget it's there.

But now, with the gigantic van
hugging the curb out front, premises
emptying systematically room by room,
standing in a corner out of the way
of burdened, grunting, shunting men you hired,
suddenly you see it, off duty and forlorn,
lying as if pasted to a floorboard.
To pick it up would just anticipate
the final sweep it waits for, harshly dinted
by its day in, day out stint of holding
steady the shelves of breakable, gilt-rimmed stuff
brought out only to gratify the in-laws.
Now with that load pampered into barrels
("Excelsior!"—the motto for all movers),
you peer along the bare floor and gauge the slant of it.
All those years the old beams went on settling.
And you, haven't you learned to settle for less?

DEGREES OF RESOLUTION

Borrowing his grandfather's reading glass
the boy next door takes time to educate us,

summoning us for safety off the grass
to squat on concrete round his apparatus,

the tool aforesaid and a random sliver
of paper. Now he tilts the glass to catch
a single dart from summer's bursting quiver,
training it on his target as we watch

to see before too long a speck of tan
appear and widen, deepen, till a wisp
of flame in scrawls too speeded up to scan
wrinkles its victim to a blackened crisp.

An odd ambivalence lies in this lens,
conferring stature on the minuscule,
hot, throbbing lines that one old gentleman's
eyes aim to see as large and still and cool,

yet of this fiercer knack an equal master,
yanking a fiery stylus down to write
a message that can only spell disaster,
culling the darker potencies of light.

Disparate ways of demonstrating strength.
The boy babbles his lecture on the laws
of optics and combustion, till at length
we back away with mumbles of applause.

The young instructor could not yet suspect
how much our nodding at his Q.E.D.
masks an uneasy leaning to reflect
on two opposing modes of scrutiny:

one that enhances to its keenest power
the lambent fact's crimped mimicking of essence,
and one whose pyrotechnics may devour

the fragile platform of their incandescence.

Rival enlightenments beneath one roof—
has one flared up to see the other fade?
Ask the old man, whose uncorrected proof
sends him out now to claim his reading aid.

A PIECE OF ROPE

It was a bad place to be a boy scout.
Tract houses huddled low on concrete slabs,
razored lawns under the pelt of sprinklers
soaked to a spongy green all summer long.
There was no place for him to pitch a tent
or light a fire. His father was away
on another trip. His mother, by contrast,
didn't seem to want to go anywhere.
Nothing to do but earn more merit badges
by developing pre-industrial skills
as advocated by the *Boy Scout Handbook*.
He sat and fiddled with a length of clothesline.
For the next badge he had to learn to tie
eight knots, and all by feel. So, he could practice
either blindfold or in some pitch-dark place.
Earlier he had tried his mother's closet.
The heat—it was July—and the packed fumes
of mothballs prickling out of garment bags
made him dizzy, and there was little room
for him on the floor hemmed in by all her shoes.
Lightheaded, lightstruck, looking for a spot
less airless (everywhere was pretty hot),

he stumbled to the patio and slumped down
on slates with ragged grass grown in between them.
(It was behind the house, not on exhibit.)

He laid the *Boy Scout Handbook* down beside him.
The cover illustration, though he'd looked
a thousand times at it, still caught his eye.
It showed a campfire in the woods at night,
with a troop elbow-crammed around it, listening
dutifully to the leader's woodlore, watching
smoke waver up, presumably not seeing
what someone with the book in hand could see:
the spectral figure of an Indian brave
hovering in a haze above their heads,
pale blue against the night sky's indigo,
part there and part not there, as if composed
at best of shifty things, like smoke and stories.
He guessed that this was meant to make him think
of the spirit of the wilderness or something.

He thumbed through pages to the knot diagram.
Overhand knots and square knots and half hitches
he could do, but what about the sheepshank,
bowline, or sheet bend? It would take some study.
After a few bouts with a kitchen towel
tied around his eyes he didn't bother,
but simply kept them shut. He knew his honor
was what he had at stake and, in this case,
honor was not too hard to satisfy.

And it was calming, hypnotizing, sitting
in his own private night with careful fingers
teaching the rope its tricks. He heard his mother
talking on the phone inside the way
she'd done ever since his father went away
on the latest trip. "No. How do I know

where he is this time or when he'll come home?
How do I know if he'll come home at all?
You know last time he said he almost didn't.
No, he doesn't call. That's different this time."
He was fumbling now; his touch was off.
He quit listening, clamping his eyes tighter.
Finally when his fingers found the loop
they needed, and he'd pulled his two ends snug,
he kept pulling, cinching the docile cord
brutally to itself. She had hung up now.

It was weeks after this that he woke up
wrenching loose from the last strands of a dream.
He was one of the scouts on the handbook cover,
but when he looked up, what he saw was no
heroic Native American but his father
leaning out of the blackness of the sky
like a new constellation, looking blue,
at once blurred and fluorescent, and unlikely
to wander down from up there any time soon.
His fingers were all twisted in the sheet
and he could hear his own voice in the dark
far away, saying over the names of knots:
throat seizing, timber hitch, lark's head, cat's-paw.
And all the rest, and none of them of much
use in the darkness he was camped in now.

AT THE BAIT STORE

Compact, uncomplicated, this is how I wish
the world could be. The only store in town,

it stocks whatever anyone would need
to stay alive, and then some—and displays it
all in one wide, dim, wooden-shelf-lined room.
Stepping past kids chugging Cokes on the porch
I jangle the strap of sleigh bells nailed to the door
and find myself beguiled by—not abundance,
but something one might call sufficiency.
Groceries, of course, but also seeds
in case you'd rather try to grow your own,
useful spools of twine, a lot of different
sizes of screws and bolts and other hardware,
plastic kites and rain capes, sunhats, snowshoes,
brooms, band-aids, ballpoint pens and glue.
Not to mention all that angling gear
that keeps the summer people popping in,
bobbers and sinkers, line, and loads of hooks.
It's all a little cluttered, but just learn
the whereabouts of each one-shelf department
and you can feel the calm of categories
soothing the mind (almost as good as fishing).
Why couldn't we live here, not just spend a week?
Like the couple of indeterminate age
who own the place, both quiet, both beneath
the low-watt lights seeming a little dough-faced
as if they never had to go outside,
only upstairs (there is a second floor,
where they must—an odd phrase—live at night).
While he counts out change with a shy smile
I can imagine how, with the cardboard sign
flipped around from OPEN to CLOSED, he pads
down for a can of tomatoes she'll be cooking,
sidling past the cash register's silence
and past the cooler where in plastic cups
of peat moss the night crawlers hibernate,
barely twitching in plugs of humus, moist
coils kept for some fair morning's hook.

CAMERA OBSCURA

It was almost too hot to move that morning.
They made love anyway, the window shade
lifted a crack to let in what little air
was stirring, or say rather simmering.
Starred with sweat, they slid apart at last
and noticed something else has found a way
through the slim aperture: a perfect image
of the sunstruck other side of their street,
spread on the white wall opposite the window
in a thin, true-colored panorama which
(as if it wasn't already odd enough)
was upside down. Everything the window
customarily framed hung topsy-turvy:
liquor and grocery signs stood on their heads,
roof antennas dangled like bare coat hangers,
and heavy drops that wept from air conditioners
rushed up instead of plummeting, like morning
dew racing to congregate in clouds.
(They couldn't see—it was out of the picture—
the sidewalk-ceiling those drops spattered on.)
This vision held for approximately ten minutes,
then faded out, leaving an ordinary,
featureless bar of white light on the wall.
They lay awhile wondering what the odds
would be of meeting such a sight again:
the angle of the sun, the set of the shade
would have to be precisely right, and they
themselves alert to serve as audience
for the unlikely, evanescent showing.
In the right place for once, at the right time!
How many happy accidents one summer morning
gathered and meshed on one hot city block
to make the humdrum world turn upside down?

FANLIGHT

A half-wheel glazed above the door:
six wooden spokes in shadow cast
increase their reach along the floor,
touching the hall's far end at last.

Deprived of full rotundity
and axle, too, on which to spin,
what else but solar energy
would fuel its daily journeys in?

Between these radiating lines
the pie-cut shapes of radiance fall.
Poured from the threshold, such designs
dazzle to shame the modest hall,

and set us squinting when our own
way in or out must cross their tracks.
Leaving the tiny torrid zone,
we feel its brand upon our backs.

You ask what all this adumbrates?
Some doors are slow to open wide.
Be hopeful, say "illuminates."
More of the same light waits outside.

LAST DAYS IN CAMDEN

I.

Days of calm. An invalid's mild diversions.
The pony cart, his present from admirers,
has the lame oldster trotting gamely round
his down-at-the-heels neighborhood once more.
It puts high color back into his face.
Jaunts of a few blocks cheer him. Reins in hand,
he tastes the freedom of a few years back,
when he could ramble far out of town, and did:
say, down the coast on a sunny winter's day
to limp sturdily up and down the beach,
tolerably like the ones he wandered
mile on mile in his Paumanok boyhood
(or like one that slips into his dreams
night after night, its flat deserted stretch
passive under the crash and yank of combers).

Summers were better still. Hospitable waters
beckoned him convalescent to the woods
back of the Staffords' farm on Timber Creek.
There he would cast his clothes aside and wrestle
with a young sapling, leaning his whole weight
against its springy stem, trying to feel
a green suppleness stealing by mere contact
into his dragging limbs.
                            He squelched in ooze
of his favorite rivulet, rinsed his mud bath off
in a clear spring, then sprawled in a camp chair
to take the sun, buck naked but for a wide-brimmed
straw hat. Slate-colored dragonflies in pairs
hovered close to his nose, inspecting him.
Sometimes he broke the silence of the woods

by singing songs he'd picked up from the army,
or from the just-freed slaves. He made
the cedars ring, an American Silenus
loafing at ease in his triumphant, improvised
western New Jersey spa. Edenic hours
penciled just as limpidly as they passed.
Casual daybook entries burgeoning into
Specimen Days. ...
                    Taking a corner now
at a terrific clip, he lurches, chuckles,
chokes up on the reins. His friends wonder:
had he ever driven before? A graybeard child,
thrilling to a new toy ...
                    Then later strokes
cut back his territory. His rig idles.
The little horse, with no way to earn his oats,
is sold at last. His outings, much less frequent,
now have to be less heady. Warren, the wiry,
mustached, cardiganed, indispensable nurse,
bumps him down to the docks in a rickety
rattan wheelchair. There he watches coal boats
smudging by, and the everladen ferry
he once rode back and forth on half the night
just to look up at stars. Tug boats mewl,
cargoes jostle on and off of barges.
All rivers are one river. Now he looks
blinking across the brown wash of the Delaware,
inhales, resigned, the air he calls "malarial."
Time to go back. His wheels jounce on pier planks.

II.

His cramped house sits on Mickle Street, an area
destitute of charm and, frankly, destitute.

An upstairs front room, homely with iron stove
and sprigged wallpaper, serves as bedroom, study,
and a salon to bands of devotees
come to receive the latest oracle.
Brash young men, the anti-Victorian vanguard,
herald his birthdays with fanatic zeal,
cosseting him with oysters and champagne.
He indulges them. He indulges himself,
as far as strength permits. Idolatry
carries vexations, though. He sags a bit
under the growing burden of their hopes
for the wonderful, unbuttoned twentieth century
that he won't live to see: a world redeemed
from priestcraft and hypocrisy, made happy
by universal suffrage and free love.
Mail will go faster (just the other day
someone sent him a little pasteboard box full
of orange buds, still fresh, from Florida).
Human relations will be governed by
the gospel of his verse and no doubt also
the wisdom of phrenology. He muses,
feeling his bumps with gentle, probing fingers.
Just as he was told: "Adhesiveness,
Amativeness, Self-Esteem, Sublimity"
all bulk large beneath his grizzled mane.

In between delphic interviews he dozes
in his big chair by the window, writes
snatches of verse, little squibs for the papers,
almost managing to ignore the reek
of the fertilizer plant across the river,
the chuff and rattle of the trains that pass
a hundred yards away and, when they don't,
on Sundays, sour Methodist steeple bells,
crass opponents of everybody's peace.
Papers and books heap round him on the floor.

He stirs them with his cane, or reaches down
now and again to riffle through the mess.
By a slow, unpremeditated system
of crossfiling, items migrate to the top.
Accolades from Swinburne, from Rossetti,
pleasant regards from Tennyson, fervent
declarations of love from female votaries
offering to conceive his child on some
fortunate mountaintop and save mankind.
Emerson's letter, lost for years, crops up,
tendering in its prim, Spencerian hand
thanks for the astonishing gift of *Leaves*:
"I greet you at the beginning of a great career."

III.

Photograph after photograph, his countenance
gives nothing away. He knows and says it:
"There is something in my nature *furtive*
like an old hen!" How many prize eggs lie
clandestine in the hedgerows of the past?
His hooded, sunken eyes at last look back
and cannot see through his own snarled webs
to find those clutches lovingly concealed.
Nor can his biographers do better:
searches for the six illegitimate children
scattered supposedly through the south yield nothing.
A mystery unto himself and others,
he lets the camera catch him if it can.

Less than a year before his death he sits
a last time for his good friend Mr. Eakins.
Paints laid aside, the savage Philadelphian
stoops under his black hood, tweaks the bulb,

and frames Walt by the window in May sunlight.
A long exposure. But the subject is
accustomed to the discipline of sitting.
Here he is Prospero with his spells disowned,
or a Hasidic sage in contemplation,
or a retired Santa Claus who seems
half-transfigured in the window-light
which sets each wispy filament of blanched
prophetic beard to glowing. He leans back
against the darker, draping shagginess
of a wolfskin, wild mate to his repose.
Spring no longer lends heat to his flesh.
He waits here, well wrapped up, for what will come.

Waits with an old lover's tingling patience.
Whatever "furtive" (his word) human fumblings
he may have hid from others, from himself,
his true secret was something else, and hidden
like Poe's purloined letter, in plan sight.
Forget the baffled courtships of young laborers,
the gifts of rings, and letters of endearment
tapering off as one by one the protégés
grew up, branched out, got married. This was not
what brought a skip and quickening to his pulse.
It was not sex but "heavenly death" which drew
his fascinated ardor all his life.
Faceless itself, reflecting all men's faces,
it held him, murmurous, many-lipped, enticing,
androgynous, a depth waiting unsounded,
into which one could slip without a ripple.
It overtook his soul in childhood,
saying its name to him on the night beach,
calling out in the tumbling of the waves.
Later it came back like a tide to steep
the rough-hewn hospitals of the Secession War.
Washed in the blood and tears of his new calling,

he sat by day and night beside the beds
of shattered soldiers, sponging at their brows,
writing their last words down in letters home.
Sometimes he helped to fold their finished hands
and walked behind the stretchers borne foot forward,
the cots already stripped for the new wounded.
Watchful, he marked the end as calm, maternal,
infinite in its welcome to desire.
This was the vision kept as counterweight
to every other force which stirred this kosmos.
So he declared his interest more than once.
Wildly out of context, for example,
in a prose dithyramb to democracy:
"In the future of these States must arise poets
immenser far, and make great poems of death."
Or is it out of context after all?
It may be just that longing for surcease,
a huge oblivion in or over nature,
which makes his writings most American.

IV.

The deathbed scene, so cherished by an earlier
century when the practice was to ebb
and cozily expire at length, at home,
played itself out on Mickle Street with some
distinctive variations. Standing in
for the extended, hand-wringing family were
disciples trading off day and night shifts,
crank journalists, male nurses, amanuenses
jotting his few words down when he could not
manage his colored pencils any more.
Appetite failed in him. The last three days
he took nothing but small sips of milk punch.

After they moved him to "a water-bed"
(startling to learn they had a thing like that
in 1892) his ragged breathing
softened, and seemed to give him much less pain.
He heard the sound of water under him
swelling and lapsing, cradling his weight,
and gave himself up to it with a smile.
It was in keeping—wasn't it?—with his style:
ample, undulant, massing and lulling back,
penned simulacrum of the sea that shaped it. ...
When he stopped breathing suddenly, his heart
("a very strong organ with him") continued
to beat ten minutes more. The camerados
watched him on his way to fathoming this:
"different from what any one supposed, and luckier."

SHUT IN

Like many of us, born too late,
(like all of us, fenced in by fate),
    the late October fly
    will fondly live and die

insensible of the allure
of carrion or cow manure.
    Withindoors day and night,
    propelled by appetite,

he circles with approving hums
a morning's manna-fall of crumbs
    hoping to find a smear

    of jelly somewhere near.

In such an easeful habitat
while autumn wanes he waxes fat
    and languorous, but not
    enough to let the swat

of hasty, rolled-up magazine
eliminate him from the scene.
    Outside, the air is chill.
    Inside, he's hard to kill.

Patrolling with adhesive feet
the ceiling under which we eat,
    he captures at a glance
    the slightest threat or chance,

and flaunts the facets of his eyes
that make him prince of household spies.
    And as he watches, we,
    if we look up, will see

a life of limits, like our own,
enclosed within a temperate zone,
    not harsh, not insecure,
    no challenge to endure,

but yet, with every buzz of need,
by trifles running out of speed.
    One day he will be gone.
    Then the real cold comes on.

PICTURESQUE

That farm just north of town
does little but subsist.
Tumbledown sheds, machines
peppered with rust: it means
another struggle to exist
is tiredly winding down.

After their stand of corn
is picked to the last ear,
they let the cornstalks stay
to bleach as pale as hay.
Signalling winter near,
beggared and blond, forlorn,

these come into their own
beneath a birdless sky,
and give the meager field
for once a second yield—
ingathered when the eye
sees beauty in the bone.

Opportunistic eye.
Eye of the passerby.

THE BOOKMARK

Tending to lose your place?
At your age you may find

a sentence (like a name, a date, a face)
escapes the ranging mind.

Stray points can be retrieved,
to which end I'm engaged
to lie at length among them, interleaved,
until you'd have them paged.

I serve as well for that
as memory serves the young.
It's no great pain to tell you where it's at
by sticking out my tongue.

A PAIR OF BOOKENDS

Two little owls, twins down to a feather,
put in hours upholding Western Civ.
Curiously, what brought them first together
holds them apart—those words by which we live.

Centered on a black marble pedestal
each of them roosts upon his open book.
Nary a hoot escapes their vesperal
calm as they brood, easy to overlook,

in a dull sheen of bronze and verdigris
guarding the upright, sober, classic row.
However distantly derived from trees,
such gathered leaves are all the leaves they know,

and would know better were they to explore

the sum of them, and not alone the ones
pinned open by their claws the while they pore.
Those folios they scan are blank and bronze,

empty reflections of their staring eyes.
I'd say they earn their space by weight and age
rather than endless hankering to be wise.
Wisdom is knowing when to turn the page.

AN ASPEN GROVE

All agitation, flinches, quiverings—
life is unrest among these skittish things.

Something gave them a scare once. In a flock
they scurried up this hillside nubbed with rock

until they reached this ridge, a firm redoubt.
Here they could take a stand, and face about,

catching their breath, still trembling. Where's their pride?
Glimpses of lily-livered underside

flitter for all to see; the merest breeze
triggers the timorous spirit of such trees

to make each leaf a manifest of fright.
Are they assailed with terror of the height

they cluster in? Or, still, of what below
routed them up the slope so long ago?

That river down there wriggles like a snake …
Why are we tempted, even now, to make

a link to legend? Manning their lookout, we're
tapping the veins of some far older fear

than any that would set us now astir.
And no, we're not afraid now. But we were.

AGAIN, CICADAS

Where were we when we heard that sound before?
Seventeen years ago these fervent minstrels,
newborn nymphs, slipped shyly underground,
while their progenitors, equally fervent,
filled summer with their bickering castanets,
clicked at a rate that rivaled the tense whine,
say, of a surgical saw cutting through bone.
Silent throughout their long novitiate
the young fattened on tree roots, served their term
as flunkies of Persephone's bedchamber.
Theirs is the longest life span of all insects,
if you can call this twilit mustering life.
But now, more than a decade and a half
outworn, they come to light, shinny up trunks,
shrug off their ragged dustcoats and flaunt wings;
all this accompanied by the ancestral music
years of muteness honed to so wicked an edge.
Noon is pressing down its stifling dome.
We cannot for the life of us remember

where, if we were together, we were sitting,
what we were thinking, feeling, or not feeling
when we were last regaled by the heady percussionists.
Isn't that all for the best? Oblivion
edits the past with a tact we've come to admire.
But periodicity still carries its pang
in pointing forward: when the next performance
batters the hot air certain trees will have gone
up in smoke, oh, ages ago, and some
who, as Thoreau said, warmed themselves twice,
first heaving the ax and finally poking
radiant ash in a blackening grate, will be
well beyond reach of that or of any heat.

MONARCHS

Enthroned on royal blue
Veronica, these two
itinerant potentates
survey their lush estates.
Day sinks to a drowse
as daintily they browse;
within their orb of flowers
the minutes might be hours,
an hour idling by
could rival all July
for slowness, stillness, heat.
The world is at their feet.

This settled state of things
is wishful thinking. Wings

that wave but to display
their poise in holding sway
will soon discover speed,
routed by pouncing need.
Rebellion in the North
will storm to sweep them forth
by ways they only know,
mourning, to Mexico,
finding a last resort
there for their exiled court.

But now they rule, at rest,
their jet and saffron crest
emblazoned on those vans
that each serenely fans.
Weed-pullers on their knees
pay tribute to their ease,
sensing the day is near
when they will not be here,
their sublime dynasty
a fluttering memory.
If memory holds worth
still on the hurtling earth
when the sedate regime
has fled and left supreme
hegemonies of ice,
let commoners think twice—
give the requisite nod
to the time's iron rod
but save their loyalty
for banished royalty.
When the warlords are slain
they will return to reign.

LUNAR ECLIPSE

She shows her brightest face
climbing the sky tonight,
then notices us edging out of place
and pilfering her light.

At first it turns her red
to find us ambling near:
could it be bashfulness or anger, spread
into her virgin sphere?

But soon her color's faded
into a paler bisque;
and now her crystal rim gives way, invaded
by our penumbral disc.

It glides aloft, occluding
all we can see of her.
So, yet again, a genius for intruding
defines our character,

and she, for once unable
to hold herself aloof
as famously had been her wont in fable,
looks down on no one's roof.

This cold, obscure conjunction,
performed, is quickly past.
We spin away, too dazed to feel compunction
at having thus trespassed,

but dragging shadow tracks
behind us like bad dreams.
Somewhere, through all of this, behind our backs,

the sun looks on and beams,

spotlighting her, still paler,
but firm in her fixed arc.
Whatever momentary shades assail her,
she dominates the dark,

and leaves us none the better
for this unlikely tryst.
Closing our eyes, we labor to forget her:
that cratered cheek we kissed,

feeling its ancient flaws
with apprehensions fed
by that bland, ascendant look which draws
the ocean from its bed.

THE LEANING TREE

Craning above the shallows of the lake
a birch tree tilts at forty-five degrees—
aberrant, ostracized by other trees
uprightly disengaged from this mistake.

Angling like a flag- or fishing-pole
but luring neither nibbles nor salutes,
this livid shaft, leaf-proud, disclaiming roots,
leans gamely after some far ebbing goal.

Mind sputters into motion, milling various
edgy expressions—"on the verge!—the brink!"—

captions imposed by one too prone to link
trumpery strands of ever more precarious

ponderings on these boughs. Their semaphore,
breezily minimal, only mimes the utter
singleness of their bent, a verdant flutter
finding no answer on the facing shore.

Can it be gesture, canted taut in search,
an attitude of beckoning or yearning?
Yield to that slant on things, and all discerning
hovers midway like this wrongheaded birch,

never quite dancing loose the drag of fact
nor tethered snug in tangibilities.
Let figures bid for pathos as they please.
See how the tree abides their sleights intact:

anchored in earth the ripples keep eroding,
the roots have not yet floated from their grip
and license trunk to jut and leaves to dip,
leaving to us the words of loss and boding.

A RECORD PRICE

(*Adoration of the Magi*, by Andrea Mantegna. Sold to the Getty Museum for $10.4 million in 1985.)

Going, going, gone ... to Malibu.
The Infant's fingers couldn't span to hold

the heavy treasures which the turbaned crew
are wishing on him, weights of spice and gold,

yet as his Mother lifts him, up he lifts
a tiny hand, accepting all he sees,
flutters a blessing on the burnished gifts
and brings the star-struck Wizards to their knees.

Such modest, mighty gestures will command
the notice of the spieling auctioneer
and bring his gavel down. Whence understand
at what a price our peace was purchased here:

Seeking his own true image, this young Lord
discerned our likeness to him, all but lost;
and knowing too how it might be restored,
he made his bid, and never grudged the cost.

DECEMBER VESPERS

Evening is early, supper too.
Moving about and stacking plates,
we notice what the windows do
when outer darkness congregates:

which is, to make a wider show
of what we've had for company—
two candles, half-consumed. They glow
in not-so-dim facsimile

on black impassive panes. They seem

to hover in the boreal air
beyond the glass, their pointed gleam
unbent by any winds out there.

Hung in a garden felled by frost,
what have they to illuminate?
Their aim and nature must be glossed;
so, of a mind to meditate,

we name them: lamps of a ruined shrine,
relighted after long disuse.
And while divided fires combine
to witness to this moment's truce

between the outdoors and the in,
we linger—less inclined to snuff
their votive lights than we had been.
Nights are already dark enough.

TO HIS PULSE

Taut, industrious little drum
tensed in the hollow of my wrist,
beating alert beneath my thumb,
nature ordains that you persist.

Even when sleep has swaddled half
the world and me with unconcern,
taps of your jungle telegraph
attend the planet's somber turn.

What's it about? The steady throb
of traffic through your narrow sluice,
a rich monotony your job
of marking time must reproduce.

On the canal around the clock
you signal with your brisk tattoo
the level reached within the lock,
drumming the vital cargo through.

That ebb and flow that you denote
returns in circles to its source;
and I, no rebel yet to rote,
am pleased to leave it to its course,

and pleased to make your paces mine,
once more to the pump and back.
Your sudden halt will be the sign
that I have left the beaten track.

THE KEY

Picking up one from the multitude ringing the maple,
I wonder why they call this thing a key:
with two stiff wings spread in a two-inch span,
green as a tree toad, it resembles more
a chloroformed, mounted specimen moth—or less
morbidly, I'd say a model glider
(or fancifully, a Japanese parrot kite).
Aerial craft of whatever kind, it's fallen

victim decisively to gravity.
I let it drop. It lunges fatally down.
Ants on forays to the disaster site
in due time will convoy scraps of wing
off to their salvage depot for recycling,
but not before the cockpit at the center
blotches brown and rends itself to spill
out of its breached care the stunned bush pilot
who at first will skulk in the tall grass,
trying to get his bearings, dazed survivor
of still another unobserved crash landing.
Now how to get back up again? It hinges
on going underground, and finding there
hiding inside him what I see I've been
rummaging for myself, the elusive key
offering entry to the sun-crossed air
as it unlocks what aims within the seed
to make its long climb upward and be freed.

FLORILEGIUM

A village crossroads; quaint, curb-hugging store.
Secondhand shelf of books: what have we here?
The Language of Flowers, by Mrs. L. Burke,
fetched down from its unobtrusive perch,
sits in the palm of a hand so delicately
you'd think it apt to flutter up and away
(if it could find a magic window open)
back to its heyday as a genteel maiden's
lexicon of the sweet codes of romance.

Look, the faded name of one who owned it
flaunts curlicues across the flyleaf: think
how eagerly she used this to construe
nosegays her young man sent her, blossom by blossom,
into the compliments he never quite
put into words as pretty as her thoughts
of what he thought of her. Of course he had
his own copy, an early gift from her.
Dutifully he consulted it, avoiding
Pink Larkspur ("Haughtiness") and Candytuft
("Indifference"), falling back on such safe bets
as Jonquils ("I desire a return of affection").
Or, as he grew in confidence, a cluster
of White Roses ("I am worthy of you").
If the bouquets became too large, she'd send
a handful of Scarlet Poppies ("Fantastic
extravagance") by way of mild reproof.

Courtship by flower telegram could take
quite a few growing seasons to be sure
that all that needed to be said was said.
To us it seems incredible, for nothing
dates faster than sentiment, except
perhaps iconoclasm. Could we salvage
any of these fair fancies for our use,
even as we forgo the parlor palms,
doilies, buttonhooks, gutta-percha collars
that furnished so unpassionately the lives
of those who spelled their yearnings out in petals?
Could we resume the perfumed ceremonies?

Small chance, seeing what makes the windowpanes
rattle just now—familiar, stuttering roar
as teen bikers in denim gun it past,
boy / girl, boy / girl, rocketing off to pop tops
in the shade of the next cinderblock 7-Eleven.

Their dust-wake coats the facing cemetery's
plastic flowers with a brusque farewell.
Where are you when we need you, Mrs. L. Burke?
Hopeless, ever to dream that fast-lane crowd,
or even we, at our more measured pace,
would pause the crack the cipher of a tongue
dead as Etruscan. ...

                  Ah, but turn the page.
Something unlooked for looks back shyly, pressed
midway through the book: a flower, in fact,
whose vital juices oozing out have left
a brownish silhouette, whose own slight form
is flatter now and drier than the leaves
it's hidden in so long. It's milky blue,
and, from its size and petals, began life as
a Violet. Which, the book says, bears the sense
of "Faithfulness." Somehow its mere survival
seems to endorse that meaning, not so different
from what those plastic blooms across the way
do their own best, in their own time, to say.

ADVANCED RESEARCH

A buzzer sounds. And now a voice, too bored
to reach for pleas or threats, broadcasts the same
old bulletin: the library will close
in fifteen minutes. I can hear a quickened
pummel of footsteps through the thin, rattling
ceiling, and I wonder what it is
holding me back from joining in the ratlike

scurry of desertion. Even more
pointedly, I wonder why I'm here.
This is a level of the stacks I've never
up to now been lost in—so far down
below ground it's in fact a sub-sub-basement.
Stingy luminosity meted out
by jittery ceiling tubes about to fail
helps even less than usual to scan
the titles moldering on their metal shelves.

Really, it's like a mineshaft; I could use
one of those flashlight caps the miners wear,
I tell myself—when, sharply as a lightbulb
switching itself on, it comes to me:
the quest is at an end. Here in this section,
if I can only find it, is the book
I've been tracking for years, beginning seven flights up,
the book that waits to tell me everything
I'll ever need to know. It's worse than hopeless
without a call number; I'm about
to give it up when suddenly my eye
fixes on a particular cobwebbed spine.
Unbelievable luck—can it be trusted?
I pull it from its shadowed perch and turn
a flaking leather cover back, and find—
dust. The pages all have pulverized
like some poor pharaoh's mummy stripped
of grave-linen in a rough hunt for gems;
now at my feet a little heap of chaff
is all this long-sought volume has to show,
except for the one smaller leaf laid in
as afterthought, printed apparently
on paper more enduring: the errata,
noted without apologies as follows:

For "inessential parts" *read* "in essential parts."

For "god" *read* "goad."
For "construction" *read* "constriction."
For "near" *read* "fear."
For "father" *read* "farther."

Settling now for anything, I pocket it.
I have five minutes left to make the door.

FINDING THE DIARY

Settling the estate, the lawyer said.
It seemed too grand a way of putting it—
bills to be paid, a bank account to close,
and finally her mother's house to sell
while her own, half-a-continent away,
sat waiting for her with its lights on timers
and neighbors dropping by to feed the fish.
Bare rooms show better, the agent said.
So she proceeded with the emptying out,
giving away most of her mother's things
to cousins for their already jammed parlors
and china cupboards, and arranged to have
one rug shipped that was too big for her car.
She even dusted, as she rarely did
at home, all the time hearing in her head
her mother's brusque, exasperated murmur
after the hired help was out the door:
"Nobody knows what clean is anymore."
Maybe, she thought, this last clean sweep would please her.
Working her way from room to thinning room,
sorting, discarding, labeling, she found

herself at last up in the attic broaching
some cartons not her mother's but her own,
packed away since she had gone to college
and her room had become the sewing room.
Sweaters gaudy with school insignia
and one, half-knitted, that she'd never finished
lay folded softly on some weightier things:
Bio and Chem notes, watercolor attempts,
the high school yearbook proving at a glance
that bliss lies in oblivion. Had she really
had names for all those eager faces inked
with urgings time had made inscrutable?
("Remember Halloween in junior year";
"Don't forget the fun we had in Art Club.")
She hurried past her own sweet, solemn picture,
then set the book aside to shuffle through
the last stack of papers when something smaller
slithered out of them in an even more
embarrassing bid for recognition. Had she
buried it there on purpose? Or just briskly
bundled it in with everything she wouldn't
want or miss when leaving home at last?
She could hardly believe that it had surfaced,
looking, unlike the rest of the sad items,
almost new—a vampire's charmed intactness—
bound in red leatherette with a gilt border,
snugged shut by a strap that snapped into
a tiny lock whose even tinier keyhole
pursed its faux-brass lips to whisper: "Psst!
I've got a secret!" It was unignorable.

The key was lost. She snipped the strap neatly
with scissors she'd been using to cut twine,
and slid herself down grimly to the floor,
her back against a blanket chest, to survey
this relic of herself at seventeen.

But there was little here, she soon found out,
about herself in isolation: Mother
vied with her for the spotlight in most scenes
and almost always took the villain's part.
The fumes of acrimony almost choked her.
To read this, you'd have thought that adolescence
was a seven-years' war. And wasn't it?
She could remember, as she hadn't wished to,
how often doors were slammed and voices raised,
or meals sat through in disapproving silence
as glacial as the silence now established
in rooms with sheet-draped furniture downstairs.
What had they fought about? What hadn't they?
Clothes, curfews, company, career,
all boiled down to combat. Would it have been
better or worse if Father hadn't died
just before these hostilities ensued?
Above the fray, he never had to take sides.
There was nothing about *him* written down
since—obviously—he couldn't be complained of,
or complained to. This was a grievance book,
pure and simple. Happy times (there were some)
had slipped by unrecorded. And it ended
in anger, as it hadn't done in life.
In recent years they'd got along beautifully,
by phone, by mail, by semi-annual visits
both of them valued. Distance was the key.
You'd never guess how well we made it up,
she thought, plodding through to the last page
where a last sentence stammered still with rage:
"Why can't she ever let me lead my own life?"

The wish was granted. Doubly granted now.
Her foot had gone to sleep. She stood and felt
its numbness augered through with pins and needles
like a sewn gash split open. All she needed

now to do was lug these boxes down
to swell the discard pile (praise the Lord,
trash pickup was tomorrow). On the landing
she glanced out at a barren autumn sky
an hour before sunset. In her own house
a time zone away, less empty, equally silent,
goldfish swiveled and lunged and nipped at sprinkled
tidbits (lucky to have obliging neighbors),
casting a flash as lights turned themselves on.

WIND AT NIGHT

A frigid midnight. For a few
slow moments, sleep eluding us,
we lie belabored by the sad,
decamping, down-and-out nomad
who makes the dark vociferous
with notice of his passing through.

As though to pangs of flesh and bone
attuned, and aching to appal,
that hapless voice so mortifies
the wincing shingles with its cries
it could well be the voice of all
the worst bereft our time has known.

Could we have thought, at this late date,
that turning pages quickly past
the planet's rash of little wars
would leave us undisturbed indoors?
When news is bad it travels fast.

Listen, it rattles at the gate,

a century's toll of traded woe.
When will it stop? We never hear,
but drift disheartened into sleep
with one storm-wearied house to keep
or to be kept by, out of fear.
Exempt, it seems, from this one blow.

THE POST OFFICE MURALS RESTORED

I'm tempted to want company to work with,
the emptiness becomes so eerie sometimes.
Locked in here after hours, clattering up
my ladder to refurbish this long, dim
lofty room I feel like the one soul
in church on a weekday (truly!) with the grilled
stamp counters filling one longer wall
like a row of unemployed confessionals,
and in place of icons, posters aimed
at stamp collectors, plus the steelier ones
reminding boys to register for the just-now-
non-existent draft, or publicizing
mug shots and fingerprints of racketeers
wanted in half-a-dozen states for mail fraud.

Mail is the point. This is a post office lobby,
I tell myself. This painted wall I'm dabbing
a mild solution of detergent on
isn't *The Last Supper*. It isn't even

anything I'd choose to paint myself—
earnest, public-minded '30s stuff—
but the artist knew what he was after
and, within limits (time and space, the ones
we all butt heads against, I'd say he got it.
In the few places where it's flaked away
to plaster my best guesses match his palette;
but for the most part it's a task of sponging,
praying the paint won't be perverse enough
to come off with the dull gray surface film.
His paint hangs firm; it rarely needs retouching.
Local color's alive under this local
dirt deposited by half a century's
cycles of winter soot and summer dust
heaved out in sighs by all who stood in line,
often wishing they could mail themselves
to where their packages would soon be going.
Jingling change in pockets, shifting weight
from one to another foot, how often did they
notice the frieze of vistas on three sides
of the room, filling space between the stone
dado and the ceiling, most of it
above eye level. Undoubtedly they saw it,
once or twice. And then, year after year,
they didn't see it. That's the way it is
with mural: make it fill the wall, it might
just as well be wallpaper. Better shrink it
and put a gilded frame around it if
you're reaching for that partly baffled hush
people assume at times in front of pictures.

What we have here is, in all, five pictures:
one on each of the shorter two side walls,
and three on the front wall broken by two windows
and the door in between that you come in by.
Coming in, of course, you don't see art

but those almighty counters that I mentioned
and, when the place is open, listless clerks,
happy only that they aren't the ones
carrying all that mail they weigh and cancel.
But if you look from side to side you'll see
a pair of facing scenes, a fated couple:
on the right, Agriculture (the real name
of this one, I'm afraid, is *Fruits of the Earth*)
and, on the left, Industry, more dryly titled
The Old Sawmill. I took these two first,
leaving the long wall with the door and windows
to fuss with later. Once I got to know them
I gave them nicknames—Ag and Ind—and found
Ind the more interesting to look at, Ag
a subtler thing to clean.

                        Ag shows a hill farm
in, I suppose, late summer, early autumn—
men are making hay in the lower right-
hand corner while the balance of the scene
is apple orchard. Big children climb ladders
while younger ones fill baskets with the windfalls.
We must be watching from a higher hill
or, like the apple-pickers, from a tree,
because the land falls back before us sloping
down even as our eyes climb higher till
the top right corner's brought us to the river
curled in like a finger crooked to beckon
the children from the trees, men from the fields.
That message hasn't gotten to them yet.
A woman in a white apron carries lunch
in a cloth-covered bucket to the hayers.
(The children no doubt sample enough apples
as not to need a meal.) It reddens me
to say it, but my delicatest care
couldn't prevent this woman's apronstrings'

dissolving at my cotton wad's fine touch.
My thinnest brush tied on the bow again,
and only I can tell. Of all the scenes
this is the simplest, but it became
absorbing once I found how many different
tints of green were underneath the grime,
from olive drab to lemon-lime chartreuse,
shadowing or highlighting a dominant
shade like the back sides of dollar bills.
(Sad, when you think how little money ever
came out of all this varied verdancy.)
The range of shading makes it less a bed quilt,
although the apples all are one unnuanced
fire engine red, and the people look
stitched in place, too static even to plod.
I think the lack of animation may
have been a planned effect, a way to hint
that here is life outside of history,
even outside of time, except for that
allotted by the seasons in their round.
You can't quite tell when any of this takes place:
the clothes are nondescript, no cars or wagons
crowd the river road. We can say only
farms like this one aren't to be found these days.

Nor is the old sawmill. This, by contrast,
offers some movement: the men working bend
with the weight of logs they shoulder, tote, and shove
into the steam-driven frenzy of the saw.
It is a great, airy, barnlike place,
with a wide-open door, through which we see
the timber wagon only half unloaded,
and an enormous, pallid heap of sawdust
kept dry under a rickety canopy. (It must
have been a product somebody would buy.)
The wagon road winds down to the same river

we saw in the farm scene, but notice, here
we're on the river's other bank, its bend
swerves outward now, more like a question mark.
Beyond, among the hills, are huddled farms
like the one we've just seen, and see no more,
that as they failed sent men down here to work.

Although in real life they'd be bored to death,
these wage-slaves are more interesting to look at
than the agrarian icons: there's the boy
of junior high school age sweeping up sawdust,
whose face needed some washing, as you'd well
expect it might on such a job as that.
Since I've gone at it (tensely, with a Q-Tip)
his cheek beams forth with such a healthy tint
it would be hard to label him exploited.
Better sawdust than chalk dust, he might say.
And there's the man on a break whittling a scrap
of wood into a doll for his daughter at home.
(Imagine how she'd say, "But where's the face?"
And he, not irritated, patient, saying,
"That's the best that I could do with that
old knife of mine. You got to draw the face on.")
What makes it more dynamic, though, is not
the figures in themselves—they're pretty stiff—
but the brisk forms they gravitate around.
Bore through the human interest and you find
circles: ironbound wheels of the wagon, fanged,
flashing wheel that is the big saw's blade,
and, not least, a great log's severed end
that faces us, clean, papery, and showing
plainly immense age. You can count its rings,
wheels within wheels that sped it to a time
when wheels would spin to bring the forests down.
Once this amount of motion is brought into it,
it's only a short step on to history.

Here, it's literally a quarter-turn,
which brings you face to face with the long wall,
full of lore to ponder on your way out.

There, as I've said, you're favored with a triptych:
a painting framing each of the two windows,
and one that flanks and crowns the heavy glass
door at the center. Would-be classical
pilasters section off these three vignettes—
it's a bit busy. Where to begin? The left,
I guess, which goes back even to pre-history,
that is, before the founding of the town.
It's of a forest clearing where a pair
of fur traders socialize with Indians.
Some small thing (a rabbit?) roasts on a spit,
and the men share a pipe beside the fire,
all wearing deerskin, though the Indians
wear less of it. It's what we'd call nowadays
a working lunch, because the trading items
are spread out waiting to be haggled over:
bearskins and beaver pelts one red man points
a finger at, while studying the beads
one of the traders holds up for inspection.
Strand on strand of colored glass; and more
spills from the open flap of the leather bag.
That isn't all: there are some useful tools
ready for swapping—needles and small knives.
No rum or guns, at least. It's fairly wholesome.
And yet ... was there a moment by the fire
when both sides could have made a better deal?
Dabbing it clean by inches I was bothered
by weird sensations, as if I could feel
the textures changing hands in these transactions.
The red men handed over something warm
and soft, and got in payment something cold
and hard. They couldn't possibly have known

what they were buying into, any more
than they or their pale guests could have divined
that this unbroken wilderness they sat in
would in a century and a bit be axed.
The trees were fair game once the game was gone.

It could be I impose the ominous tone.
Look without thinking too much and you see
something innocuous as boy scout camp.
At the far right, though, is a view that doesn't
force you to work at reading danger into it.
This is a night arrival at a station
of the Underground Railroad. Runaway slaves
bend double, scuffling down the cellar steps
of the red-bearded parson who became
a local legend: here he is, presiding,
grim in his clericals with a covered lantern,
holding his cellar hatch up for the last
passengers that hustle through his barnyard,
trying to beat the moon before it rises
over the cloud it just peeps out from now.
The scant, worrying light it sends down hits
the parson's face, set in an anxious scowl,
showing more plainly than the faces of
his no doubt equally anxious overnight guests.
If not their features, plenty of their fear
comes through in the forward lunge of bodies
into the battened safety of that hole.
This Henry Ward Beecher of the provinces
stuck by his own moonlighting, shunting hundreds
in here and out, and off to Canada.
These Blacks are in every sense just passing through.
There are no Blacks in town now that I know of.
(Nor, you'll be thinking, any Indians. Right.)

Finally I'm at the final scene, the aegis

under which all must come in and go out.
I've set my ladder up astride the door;
if we were open and you wanted stamps
you'd have to risk bad luck and weasel under it.
(Another reason to do this job at night.)
Of all the paintings this is the most crowded,
and yet it seems of all of them the most quiet.
Memorial Day is what it's called. It gives
a view of the town green, a small triangle
of grass and a few trees and a generic
Union Soldier's statue at the center.
It's a mass gathering, a chance to wear
a uniform if you have one, or just dress up,
parading to and from the cemetery,
ending up here, after the wreaths are laid,
for the Mayor's speech, more drumrolls, more salutes.
See how they stand in neat rows round the statue
like the redeemed that throng a reredos
before the Throne of Grace: the Volunteer
Fire Department, all six of them, and one
policeman standing close behind the Mayor;
schoolchildren holding tiny flags and staring
at all the former doughboys who've been home
now for more than a decade from the War
to End All Wars. One's missing an arm. Many
show a middle-aged spread. They all stand tall
in khaki for a day. This is how things were
when it was painted, fifty years or so
ago, and it is here that history
comes to an end in this small town P.O.
Silence and night press in against me now.
Try as I will, I can't dream up the sound
of the small band, of the determined voices
singing "There's a long, long trail a-winding,"
nor of the huffed, triumphal rhetoric
disgorged beneath the statue's stony trance.

This one-armed man I'm sponging off looks happy,
as they all do—just happy to be home.
When I go home myself, fold up my ladder,
and leave by this glass door for the last time,
I'll notice as I always do the neat stroke
of wit the artist realized in his placing
a view of the town center *at* the center:
for, whenever I step outside, I see
in front of me the place itself: the grass
triangle with its statue just the same,
most of the same trees (though some elms are gone)
and the same modest downtown row of stores,
shabbier now, some seven recessions later.

To go out from his painting, then, should be
to step inside it, to become a part
of what you've just been looking at. It must
have made the townsfolk back then smile and think,
"This place is ours, inside and out," and think
that even the worst troubles might be managed.
I wish it were that easy, every night
when I lock up and walk across the green
to midpoint where, feeling myself inspected,
I slow my pace under the sentry's granite
stare from his high pedestal—too high
for me to look him straightly in the eye,
as I have done so often with his twin
inside, up on my ladder. College boys
who, when they're home for Christmas every year,
sneak out at night to crown him with a ski cap
have met his level gaze on his own level.
I can no more make out his hard young face
than I can see that of the figure slumped
across the street in the bus shelter, where
he's found himself a home to last the night.
What made our muralist omit that sight

and others like it which his Great Depression
furnished in plenty was, I'm now persuaded,
not an genteel aversion to the worst
sores and unrest a nation had to show
but a belief that they would not be lasting,
a flash of confidence. Why can't we share it?
Too much has happened since those old hard times.
Three wars and fifty-odd Memorial Days
after the painter laid his brush down, I
take pains to cleanse and blot his bristling strokes
that aimed to smooth the wrinkles of the world,
and inch by inch unveil their earliest gleam.
But walking home through streets that night has emptied
in this small town that's never come to much,
those heartening hues are hard to bear in mind.
I see cast over all what I would paint
if I were ever given the commission:
that dinginess hope leaves when it deserts us,
that smudge of squandered opportunity.

From *Below the Surface* (1999)

For Hilary

PAPER BIRCH

When we were children, summer's endless search
for things to do would lead us to the birch

that stood like something conjured up with chalk
between your driveway and your gravel walk.

The outer skin that ravels off in rolls
we peeled away and commandeered for scrolls

on which we scribbled with a pencil stub
code messages about our secret club.

Who could unriddle what they meant? We skewed
ciphers so much they couldn't be construed

even by us from day to day. We grew
up and away from that; before we knew,

away from one another. Decades passed,
leaving not much to glean from this at last,

alone in my own yard. But there's a tree
doing a fair job as facsimile,

shedding its bark to paper over gaps
from there and then to here and now. Perhaps

I should accept its hint, investigate
where you are now. It might not be too late

to take advantage of the tempting white on it.
As you can see, I'm still inclined to write on it.

12:00 M

High summer pauses overhead.
Taking a breather in its climb,
the sun neglects to mark the time.
The faintest shadow of its tread
has vanished with the morning breeze.
A static hush prevails. The trees

are hulks of leafage, unimpelled.
The heavy earth's hot atmosphere
has fluttered to a standstill here,
a single breath drawn in and held,
as though in wonder or in fright,
looking down now from some great height.

How can a moment be this slow?
The whole yard clenches in suspense.
Then, from a weed clump by the fence,
a cricket chirps a signal: *Go*.
And the gold marcher, none too soon,
steps down from noon to afternoon.

BACKYARD ARCHEOLOGY

These little medicine bottles I dig up
every time I lengthen a flowerbed
lead me to think this area was a dump
for the farmhouse that stood here way back when.
Too small to use again for anything,

they got jettisoned as the pining residents
sampled cure after inexpensive cure,
figuring to stave off the doctor's visit.
Patent remedies, and for the most part patently
ineffective. Now their emptied vessels
sparkle modestly up from shoveled clods.
Most often flat, round-shouldered and short-necked,
they seem always to lack their caps or corks.
The molded letters, although etched and clouded
by dirt and gravel, still are legible,
advertising names that once stirred confidence.
Folks with not much to invest in illness
founded their hopes on following directions:
ten drops four times a day for their neuralgia.

Sitting by spoon and cup and water jug,
these furnished the stunted, make-do sickrooms
which I can see in flashes now, dislodging
this new specimen from my latest spadeful:
the enforced hush, children chased from the threshold,
the women stationed all night at the bedside,
bending with cold wrung cloths to pacify
Hiram or Hannah, tossing in such a fever
the bed-ropes loosened. Think of the processions
up and down the narrow, steep backstairs
with chamberpots, with fresh or soiled linen,
with covered mugs of clear broth or beef tea.
The screenless windows always shut at night,
the white net curtains blurring out the sky.
The ceiling cracks that to the fevered eye
coalesced in scenes of mystic import:
long-gone relatives beckoning over Jordan.
"Mother and Father—aren't they looking young! ...
Is that a bird singing? It sounds so close,
it sounds like something right here in the room."
(Out in the hall the children strained their ears.)

"Why is it getting dark so suddenly?
Isn't it just the middle of the day?"
(The women watching couldn't think what to say.)

Marshaling what poor weaponry they had,
including drops from these obliging flasks,
they fought it out against a flock of ailments
no longer heard of, which you'd almost think
departed with the disadvantaged patients:
phthisic, catarrh, brain fever, bloody flux.

Squat neck chipped, this latest artifact
has the accustomed shape, bringing to mind
one of the two Tables of the Law
or the plain headboard of a child's bed.
Now that I've wiped the moist earth off of it
I see it's an odd color, a faint blue.
I hold it like a reading glass, look through
and see the growing garden stricken wan
with some archaic malady—still lingering
and potent in these out-of-the-way parts?
And now there's not a drop of this once prized
elixir left, whose diligent consumers
are equally beyond recall, confirmed
in what they came to guess with each new twinge:
that in the end there's only one sure cure.

THESE DAYS

Our cat, who knows no better,
goes hunting in the dawn.

Hair-trigger nerves abet her
as she patrols the lawn,

slicking back ears and whiskers
to pin her nose to scents
of injudicious friskers,
seed-eating innocents.

Chipmunks and mice most often
(but once, a star-nosed mole)
have waltzed into the coffin
by stepping from the hole.

The same unvaried format:
her latest cause to crow
lies stiffening on the doormat;
the kitchen radio

competes for our attention
with its own body counts.
A matter of dimension,
a matter of amounts,

I think, and drop the victim
gingerly in the trash.
The destiny that picked him
to exit in a flash

is now all plush and languor,
rolling in sunny grass.
She slaughters without anger,
incorrigible, alas;

nothing will ever get her
to mend the universe.

Truly, she knows no better.
(Notice, she does no worse.)

LOW TIDE

You'd think the sea with all its busy rollers
would wipe out every wrinkle it could reach.
Not so: for here, exposed to weekend strollers,
is low tide's broad and corrugated beach,

runnelled and gray and ribbed like an old washboard.
The saturated, packed, uneven sweep
is wonderful underfoot as we walk toward
shallows stampeding back to bloat the deep.

It's a world flung wide open. We can wander
widely at will across this crimped terrain
of cryptic pleats and scorings left to ponder.
What can the cunning fissures of the brain

gather from lines decamping waves dashed off?
"Ordered away—full explanation follows"?
That would suffice, as each brigade splashed off
to swell the ranks amassed in those cold hollows.

Now the tide's turning in (it seems) slow motion.
Winking between these miniature dunes
are finger lakes of foam and brine the ocean
left to preserve a foothold. Afternoon's

ebbing. All that water wrote on sand

will fall to water's next clockwork invasion.
There will be more of water, less of land.
Maybe in time we'll glimpse the full equation.

ON THE FOOTBRIDGE

Clutching the rail, bent heads studious, blond,
my son and daughter drop a yellow leaf
(one of a number lately come to grief)
into the spillway draining from the pond,

tracking its wet, unwilling fall from grace,
rapt in the spate of water joggled white.
But at the bottom, look, it comes to light
passing from havoc to a milder pace,

tacking this way and that, a tiny raft
of torchlight on the sepia of the stream.
As though its dipping had enhanced its gleam,
it flickers hotly, bobbeting fore and aft,

blinking away at last around the bend
where the woods cast a thick avernal shade.
Picture it moored where none will see it fade.
What sort of trees will overlook its end?

Those here in sight have progeny to spare—
hardly would miss one scattered son or daughter.
There I would differ. Turning from the water,
I watch the sun flash off the children's hair.

HALFWAY

That tree close to the road
burns red where it looks north.
Half of its sap has slowed,
making it glow in shame
or fury colder nights have goaded forth.
Time only is to blame.

The southern-facing boughs
are green as any summer's
opulent heat allows.
Half Burning Bush, half Tree
of Life! Its limbs hold something for all comers,
a ripe dichotomy,

bearing a balanced freight
of growth and of decay,
two emblems of its fate
sprung from the same hard wood.
There we can see both seasons thrive, and say
each in its turn is good.

Another night or two
will spark the rest ablaze,
showing the inner hue
of all that time destroys.
So much can be expected. While it stays,
treasure the equipoise.

ON A BIRTHDAY

Your heights, recorded year
by year on the doorframe—
it shows how little we're
allowed to stay the same,
a ladder my eyes climb
in efforts to recall
penciled-off tracts of time.
Scattered and vanished, all
but memory's residue:
a cobweb of designs
that clings to these ruled lines
but can't encompass you.
By increments as steady
as minutes sifting by
you move from our Back Then
into your Here and Now,
not yet wondering why
or having to worry how.
Up and up; you'll stop,
you say, when you're good and ready.
What's up there at the top
neither of us can see,
have nothing to see with:
your own allotted zenith.
I hope that it will be
better than worth your while,
something you can justly
take the measure of
without regret, with neither
too much or little love.

Meanwhile, back to counting.
Another line drawn—there.

You turn and look and laugh
at line on line amounting
to one poor, homemade graph
of time we mark together.
It's one we're pleased to share.

GETTING FARSIGHTED

The latest news from here?
Distance is wearing thin.
Far off is inching near,
and taps to be let in.

Road signs, once a blur,
have never been so bold.
The clock-thermometer
now beacons hot or cold

with punctual blatancy
from high atop the bank—
unwonted clarity
for which time is to thank.

Fine print, old intimate,
has grown standoffish, though;
held out at arm's length, it
repeats what I should know,

this line of Blake's: "The eye
altering alters all."
I peer up at the sky,

unlikely yet to fall,

but sagging here and there
as here and there change place.
Time's presbyopic stare
reorganizes space.

OLD ADDRESS BOOK

Handily thumb-indexed, my alphabet
of friends with all their out-of-date addresses
is something I thumb through with some regret.
Some of their whereabouts are simply guesses.

Erstwhile colleagues, classmates, confidants—
just when did we stop writing? And just why?
Caught in the listing of their former haunts,
it's more than memory, with a valiant try,

is able to retrieve. This couple split,
she has the children, he went—somewhere. Where?
(Some have dropped out in ways more definite,
leaving their lawn work to perpetual care.)

As to the few I hear from, I can see
in altered entries under every name
the upward trudgings of mobility.
Look at the moves it took to play the game:

the better neighborhood, the better job,
the better climate sirened them away,

taking a mere half-dozen years to rob
the ragged book of half its use. Today,

after I'd copied out the ones still good
I thought I would discard this now unneeded
dogeared directory. And so I should,
were I not stunned by all that's superseded.

NIGHT LIGHTS

When I was small and went to bed
the ceiling sloped above my head.

The room was dark, the curtain thin.
I saw the headlights hurtle in

to whip across the inner wall
and scale the ceiling, through a sprawl

of shadow from a clothes-draped chair.
Then they were gone. I wondered where.

Sometimes I huddled at the sill
to watch them veering close, until

they lashed their way inside the room.
Was it a message? Meant for whom?

If I looked up I saw the stars:
less flashy than the lights of cars,

less hurried, less inclined to poke
into the eyes of dozing folk;

nonetheless ready to confer
directions on the traveler

who, led astray by his own lights,
could wander lost for many nights.

That, of course, isn't what I said
then, when the stars saw me to bed.

Not here and gone but here to stay,
they made their point a subtler way,

by a slow, pulsing enterprise.
To see them now, I close my eyes.

MAN WITH METAL DETECTOR

You know me. I'm the one
who isn't dressed for the beach,
arriving late in the day
when you're folding your umbrella
or shaking out your towel.
I must look from a distance
like some insane slave-laborer
tasked with tidying up
as much sand as I can
with some pathetic tool, some
peculiar carpet sweeper.

In fact what this picks up
is hid below the surface.
I put its ear to the ground
and when, from inches under,
it hears the note, inaudible
to me, of something metal,
the needles on its dial
shiver to full attention.
Then I use my grandson's
shovel to excavate.
Sometimes a soda can,
sometimes a dime or quarter,
sometimes even jewelry
(though more of that turns up
in playgrounds and in parks
than down here by the ocean).
It's more like prospecting
than like archeology.
Unwittingly let slip
or purposely discarded,
these relics offer few
hints of their past owners:
a lost coin is every
bit as anonymous
as a chucked beer tab.
Once in a long while
I come across initials.
It gives me a bad feeling.
I don't really want to know
who *M. S. M.* is, whose ring
I picked up near the boardwalk.
Eighteen-caret gold
and set with a seed pearl.
Smaller than all my fingers.
Was it loose on hers?
Did she put it in a pocket

which then proved treacherous?
Or (and this is worse) did she
strip it off and throw it
to rid herself of someone
she got it from, someone
she would have liked to see
thrown down hard and buried?
My Sad Monogram,
what's the use of asking?
You've long since found out
insurance didn't cover it,
or if you meant to lose it
you didn't even ask.
Pardon me for making up
your story from such meager
evidence—it shows how
things turning up these days
turn naggingly suggestive,
won't leave my mind the way
I want it: matter-of-fact.
Something about this hobby
is getting out of hand.
I only took it up because
the doctor wants me walking.
I feel like knocking off
sooner than usual today
and simply sitting awhile
to watch the way the tide
oversteps itself in long
rippling strides of silk,
making a cleaner sweep in time
than any I could make.

PROSCENIUM MASKS

Colleagues, antagonists, *dramatis personae*
stylized, stark, and trophy-hung on high,

framing the action, upper left and right,
each in his corner flaunts on opening night

full-blown catharsis in a carven face,
summits of feeling strictly out of place

in any place we commonly frequent.
Here they pursue their deadlocked argument,

one with a tortured countenance of woe,
the other ravaged by a wild ho-ho.

Knowing ourselves unlikely to endure
any emotion quite as simon-pure,

we sit between them and suspend belief,
drawn to one's merriment, the other's grief

as comic or as tragic scenes ensue.
Prompters who only know a single cue,

they can be overlooked as we explore
levels of empathy we'd missed before,

charmed by illusion till the final curtain
closes on what the final act made certain.

Houselights are up; we're up. And there abide
the impassioned features never modified,

urging a question: Could the mightiest play
make us emote as ardently as they?

And could our nerves sustain it? Why not ask,
while we're about it, what's behind each mask?

Wondering thus, we wander up the aisle.
Behind our backs the two lament and smile,

seeing us out to where our undramatic
lives offer joys and sorrows less emphatic,

not as well-plotted and, above all, cursed
by having to be gone through unrehearsed.

A MICA MINE

Curiously, we don't go down but up
to get into it—up a gravelly path
leading us to the scooped-out top of this
modestly-sized mountain. It's more a quarry,
really, than a mine, a man-made
miniature box canyon. Looking up
the rock walls in their horseshoe curve
we see the sky burn with a fiercer blue
along the granite rim, the way it will,
paling, cooling as our eyes climb higher
into its cloud-free loft. Conceive a view
from the bottom of a wide, drained rain barrel:
and in fact the worn stone floor we stand on
is basined here and there by shallow, amber

puddles from a recent rain. No shafts
tunneling into the sides, but an assortment
of alcoves, only big enough to step into,
trading the sky-roof for an overhanging
rock-roof. They suggest a vanished tribe's
feeble attempts at tombs or living quarters
that went nowhere.

                The mine has been worked out
for decades. People come, like us, to pick up
souvenir shards of the last mineral product
that made someone a profit here. The mica
lies scattered all around, the largest heaps
close to the rock-face. Weightless and translucent,
abandoned casually, a long-departed
giant's nail-parings. Seriously, though,
they would have used a lot of this for panels
set in the doors of parlor stoves, through which
the cloistered flame would give a waxy glow.
"Isinglass"—wasn't that what they called the stuff?
Hold a scrap up to the sunlight and you'll see
nothing with clarity, but a diffused light
that wavers in the crystal's web of veins,
at once bright and frustratingly unfocused,
like something lost in the past half-reappearing
but slipping back before it can be named.

There doesn't seem to be much more here to see
in a spot so bare and quiet that a beaked,
cruciform shadow drifting past our own
late morning short ones brings a shiver. Now
is one of those moments when we wouldn't mind
having one of those stoves to huddle round
with its pane of mica offering a view
of fire tamed and fed and dutiful,
helping us to forget, perhaps, just how

greatly alone and questionably placed
we are here at the bottom of the sky.

AN EXHUMATION

(Elizabeth Siddal Rossetti's)

I.

Spades jab and scoop in the night mists
of Highgate Cemetery. Somber-coated
witnesses stand clustered in the flare
of oil lamps. Iron strikes wood. They raise
the narrow box and haul it to the gatehouse,
feeling the weight not only of the tenant
but damp infused by seven years below ground.
They pry the lid up. Someone's black-gloved hand
fumbles inside to free from buried tresses
(Deep golden locks, her sovereign coronal)
the buried book, a volume of gray calf.

No, not a vampire movie, just an aberrant
cultural milestone, 1869.
The poems, put there by the hand that penned them,
in expiation of whatever part
their author played in triggering suicide,
would prove at length, predictably enough,
a loss the widower could not endure.
Repent in haste, rationalize at leisure.
Finally he pulled the necessary strings,

secretly obtaining the Home Secretary's
quizzical sanction of this evening's work
(carried on in the edgy poet's absence
by his astonishingly duteous friends).

Having confirmed they had the proper book
(Christina had slipped in a Bible also),
they went about resettling in the ground
one they agreed was stunningly preserved—
perhaps the laudanum that swirled her off
had locked her tissues in some eerie stasis?
It was the face they'd seen so many times.

Before they brought the gray book to Rossetti
one of them sprayed it well with disinfectant.

II.

It was the face they'd seen so many times
haloed by gilded frames, her flowing hair,
a red-gold wonder, flaming round her pallor.
Milliner turned model, she became
Beatrice to Rossetti's Dante, drifting
soon into other canvases than his.
She lay in sodden costume in a bathtub
to pose as drowned Ophelia for Millais.
When the gas heaters underneath went out
she nearly froze, said nothing, playing dead.

Lizzie, "the Sid," "the stunner," or to her
Intended, cozily, "Guggums"—she impressed
Ruskin enough with her own poems and paintings
to wheedle from him an annuity.
The doleful watercolor that she did

of the churchyard in Wordsworth's "We Are Seven"
hung for years in her doctor's dining room.
The face her painter-poet-husband painted
gazes opaquely, fatal, fragile, sphinx-like:
those heavy-lidded eyes, those chiseled lips
never will tell us what led things to curdle
between her and Rossetti. The engagement
yawned on for years, the marriage when at last
it came about was brief. A stillborn child,
a horde of bodily and mental ills
challenged her husband's flagging chivalry,
turned it to something cooler and evasive—
an urge to shun engulfment by the glum
undertow of her extreme self-pity,
the regular descents into hysterics
that nothing short of laudanum would calm.
The last repulse: he walked away one evening
for a few hours from their shared miasma.
When he came back he found her silenced by
the bottle she had drained of all its stupor.
"Accidental," said the Coroner's Jury.
Rossetti, though, could read the overdose
for what it was: the whiplash of a Fury.
His own sleep after that was nightmare-cursed,
or mimicked hers, the grudging boon of drugs.

III.

One thinks of her, disdainful damozel,
flinging scorn from the gold bar of Heaven:
"*Take* the precious poems! I never asked for them!"

One thinks of him, transcribing in a sweat,
not venturing to ponder much the hole

that ravaged half a stanza on one page.
Restored, it meets our eyes in glossed editions.

We read the lines bemused as usual
at what will not stay buried—and what will,
only to flourish strangely in the tomb:
sourceless light vibrant as grace or fault
Like fiery chrysoprase in deep basalt.
Brooding on this, he wrote as one who knew:
Even so much life endures unknown, even where,
'Mid change the changeless night environeth,
Lies all that golden hair undimmed in death.

So it was wasted delicacy of feeling,
his friends endeavoring not to let him know
what it appears he pictured then and often:
how Lizzie's hair, snaring his derelict words,
had kept on growing till it filled the coffin.

THE CRAYONS

On the first day of school they gave them out,
the basic pack of eight. Lifting the flap
we ran our fingers over the pristine
conical tips and sniffed the freshly milled
petrochemical fragrance they gave off.
Soon enough they would be worn to nubs,
their paper sleeves peeled back as they diminished,
spreading their substance on the grainy paper
we were allowed (invited!) to mess up.
But what we drew in fact was steeped in order.

We were a school: we had our pet conventions.
It was as though each stick of color had
subjects (or do I mean *objects*?) coded
deep in its waxy bowels, which without
much aid from us could put themselves on paper:
blue was for sky, a ribbon that we stretched
across the top inch only of the page;
green for grass and cotton wads of leaves
we put on tops of trees, brown for their bark
and for our fathers' briefcases and shoes.
Out of the red crayon came our mothers' lips
and apples always ripe upon the tree;
the purple one made thunderclouds and grapes
and plushy velvet robes for kings and queens.
Orange, of course, for pumpkins, black for cats
and witches' capes and curlicues of smoke
that spewed like broken bedsprings from the stacks
of coal-fired locomotives on the move.
The sun, a yellow knob that bristled smartly
with lollipop sticks of the same yellow,
looked down on all of this and called it good.

Of course, we know now it was all wrong.
We never could have lived long in those houses
with perfect triangle roofs and no rain gutters.
Our visions of the world had no perspective—
things meant to be in back appeared above—
and they were innocent of shading, too.
The colors of the rainbow, plus a few,
were all we ever needed: beige or taupe,
aqua, magenta, coral, slate, or maize
were ours yet to discover with the thrill
of shopping for our own bath towels and sweaters.
By the time we grew into the bigger
box of crayons (featuring white for snow,
gray for Grandma's hair, and that odd color

all of us then unblushingly called "flesh"),
we had tiptoed into a truer style.
Copying carefully, we learned to roll
the sky down like a classroom map to press
tightly on the horizon, and we started
to make things small that were far off from us,
and dulled the light of what we drew with shadows.
Smiling, the teachers marked our progress.
Stripped of its spokes, the sun withheld its praise.

TIME-LAPSE PHOTOGRAPHY

Those television nature films you watch
when nothing else is on are slaves to it,
as you yourself become, beguiled by
the heady briskness of such overviews,
shuttling seasons through on celluloid,
mounding or melting snowbanks in an instant.
Magically fast the rosebud opens wide
its damask folds and poses for a close-up;
apples ruddy themselves and corn stalks rocket,
and, as you blink, the maple leaves trade in
their August green for their October bloodbath.
Small contractors culminate their designs
as quickly as they pounce to ambush prey;
in a few seconds anthills tower up
or spiderwebs are spun and decked with dew
and open for grim business. Honey bees
mold and fill their wax hexagonal vats
rapidly as a cannery conveyance belt.

Cornering interest by accelerating
what would complete itself in any case,
the trick appeals to your peculiar urge
to see how things turn out that commonly
wouldn't come close to catching your attention.
It's over in an hour: life goes on
in front of the now silent, darkened screen,
conforming to a pace no cameraman
would undertake to alter. Notice, though,
how much earlier now, at summer's ending,
the windows of the room become opaque;
and as you switch the lamp on, notice too
that brown spot on the back of your left hand—
plainly there for the first time you remember,
looking, for all its suddenness, right at home.

THE PORCH SWING

It was what other people would have called
a glider—but to them that would have meant
an engineless airplane. So they always said
the porch swing, though it had no ropes or chains
to swing from, this scaled-down divan of sheet metal.
It slid (glided?) to and fro in a frame.
A set of springs and shifting balance did it.
There was a sound the springs made, not too loud,
but intimately keyed to summer evenings.
Not a mere rusty squeak, more like a high
fretted steel guitar string being plucked.
They must have liked the effect; they'd never
oiled it away in all those years.

Silent themselves, they let it speak for them,
slumping back in it, waiting for the air
to shrug off heaviness, casting their own weight
away in cradle rhythm. Twilight turned
to deeper tones of twilight. When I try
to place myself, I'm lower down and farther
forward, sitting on the splintery steps,
breathing in the ground's hot jungle smell,
watching with all my ponderous attention
for the first firefly to show itself.
Then I would see one, then another. More. …
Their lovely small escapes from gravity
shimmered up from the darkened grass, and then
the thin metallic note rising behind me
was just the sound their sparks would have produced
if they were aimed at ear as well as eye.

HIDE-AND-SEEK

Under the table was no good. The cloth
hung down at most halfway. Behind the sofa
two friends were already huddled. She could hear
her brother on the back porch counting down—
"… three, two, one"—and just before
his bellowed "Ready or not, here I come"
she dove into the closet under the stairs.
Not much bigger than a telephone booth
and with a ceiling sloping to the floor,
it was a catch-all bin for hanging coats
(or slickers, once the coats were coffined up
in cedar for the summer) and for stowing

items lacking obvious spots to be in.
The vacuum cleaner and the croquet set
claimed much of the floor space. There were a few
stacks of the magazines her mother meant
to read sometime before they were thrown out.
She sat down quietly on one of these
and let her eyes grow more used to the dark.

It wasn't totally dark in any case:
there was a glowing finger's-width between
door and floorboard, and from the keyhole
an even brighter wizard's wand was jabbed,
searching into the farthest reach of shadow,
solid-looking, pencil-thin, unfaltering,
tempting to put a fist around except
it looked white hot enough to leave a brand
on any flesh it touched. (She knew it wouldn't,
but kept hands off it anyway.) She stared
at jumpy, moiling motes of dust it harried
out of invisibility and held
in its suspended corridor for inspection.
Once she had asked her mother, "Where does dust
come from?" and her mother, dusting, said,
"I declare, I think it comes from you."
Could it be true? She peered at the minute
and witless midair antics. Then she felt an itch,
and quietly, because by now she heard
footsteps and giggles of others being found,
she rubbed mosquito lumps around her ankle.

Under her pumicing fingers she could feel
smidgens of something crumbing from the surface—
the summer's grime? Or her own skin, somehow
more friable than she'd assumed? The thought
of turning into dust by merely rubbing
herself away, being her own eraser,

grain by grain becoming part and parcel
of the unresting flurry she now gaped at,
gripped her. For the lit-up mites she saw
there were a multitude she couldn't see:
they were what the dark air touching her
all over now was full of. When her brother
finally got wise and crept up soundlessly
to the shut door and slid a gleeful thumb
over the keyhole, terror tripped a switch
deep in her throat, and the scream she came
bursting into the light with scared him, too.
So when she reached out to him, he was rattled,
said not to be silly, slapped her wrist,
and ran away, yelling that she was It.

ON THEIR ANNIVERSARY IT RAINED

and when they got back from the restaurant
and he was finished mopping off the sill
of the window they'd left open, he fell into
thinking about the way they used to stand
on the little, tacked-on screened porch, back
in the earlier house, to watch the thunderstorms
tossing down rain and lightning (lots of it,
there on the coast)—and how, in the stark flash
of those discharges, water caught in the screenmesh
would gleam remarkably, a grid of opals,
and rain on the thin roof would carry on
nearly as grand a pummeling as thunder,
and all around a scoured, half-rusty smell
interlaced air and water. When he asked her

if she remembered that, she told him yes,
she thought about it sometimes. They could feel it
freshening the air then (miles inland,
and despite days and nights gone down the spout)—
another of those things they had in common.

ICE TIME

Now winter bares its teeth.
Fang upon dripping fang
festoons each overhang.
As we duck underneath

on our way out or in
we ask, Will this portcullis
flash down to annul us?
It is no friendly grin

the roofs and gutters show.
You say one willing vandal
swinging a shovel handle
would end the threat. I know,

and yet I hesitate.
Something in this grimace
that wracks the season's face
disposes me to wait

at least a while, to see
how much the sun can do
by sending daylight through

the jaws of jeopardy.

If, dazzled then, I leave
the long points gleaming there,
call it a child's dare
flung at the bristling eave

just for the hell of it.
We have crossed thresholds more
beset by risks before
and lived to tell of it.

SPECIMEN STARFISH

Out of your element, decorating mine,
skeletal, pale, you have your points (all five).
Years have gone by since, pirating the brine,
you practiced savagery to stay alive.

Thoroughly dried and cured, a rigid pith,
with nothing more to do than radiate
five ways at once, the arms you do it with
are nothing fearful now to contemplate.

To run a finger down their tapered length
offers no inkling of their tensile skill—
how fathoms down their suppleness had strength
to ravage clam and oyster shells at will.

As to that stomach you would then extrude,
enveloping the prey it would digest,

one has seen daintier ways of downing food.
Now, like your arms, your empty hub's at rest.

To roam the sunken terraces, to feed,
to slither out of reach of greater jaws,
to mate in season, profligately breed—
these were your appetites, your only laws.

Fish out of water, star late of the sea,
why do I keep you stranded on my desk?
Perhaps to show how unconcernedly
I can share surface space with the grotesque?

No, it goes deeper. Distance from the deep
narrows as I address my risen star.
Haven't I felt, half-foundering in sleep,
the tidal strains that made you what you are?

FIRST BIRD

Two mornings running—or does this make three?—
I've suffered from this bird's precocity.

Like a raw chorister who's jumped the gun
he sings before the faintest touch of sun

powders the deeper dark to deep twilight.
If he can see an end at hand for night

he's sharper-eyed than I am. When the flocks
join in, they sound aggrieved. Perhaps their clocks

synchronize more with mine than his, or they
assume a warier mood in meeting day.

Count me with them, although I know, of course,
that little syrinx can't evade the force

goading it on to jubilate alone.
Why should I take exception to the tone

twittering up from instinct's feathered pawn?
Briefly I do, then drowse from dark to dawn.

ANOTHER ORPHEUS

I sounded the last string;
my voice came to a stop
on an affecting quaver
only half intentional.
Shaken, the dark king
gave his assent,
set free this one of his
lately arrived bondwomen.
There was no precedent.

Up the hushed ramps
of basalt never swept
by wind, but crisscrossed
here and there by little
creeks, escaping trickles
from rivers overhead,

up, up we climbed,
she, mute, half-slumbering
still on the arm of Hermes,
while I, used to following
her quick steps everywhere,
found myself in the lead,
sworn not to look at her
until we both stood clear
of the avernal mouth.
I thought, *Once we're back
in the light of day my songs
all will be of her.
Her every gesture,
the least turn of her head
will call forth my words;
and my words will look to her
to be their living proof.*
Ducking past rock-teeth
jutting from the roof,
I kept my gaze straight,
straining toward the door
not yet come into view.

We came on it suddenly:
the grade evened out,
the path took a final
twist or two and then
the dazzling upper world
was a bare stride ahead,
rock-framed, awaiting
our first reborn steps.
Behind me I could hear
her startled, indrawn breath,
and the vista pulled my hand
up in the air to point.
"Look," I cried, and she,

darting under my arm,
plunged out into the sun—
and turned to see me stunned,
still behind the threshold,
sealed from her eager reach.

She saw me drop away,
my flesh turning vaporous
even as hers grew firm.
I saw her outstretched hands
(the last bright thing I saw)
groping after nothing as
I sank back to the deep
throne chamber of Dis.
Hermes Psychopompos
steadied me by the elbow,
announced me as before.
Truly they welcomed me,
unsurprised as they were.
Now I sing for the court.
All my songs are of her.

A GEODE

For Peter Olenchuk

What started out a glob of molten mud
hawked up by some Brazilian volcano
back in the Pleistocene is now a rock
of unremarkable appearance, brown

as ordinary mud and baseball-size.
Picking it up produces the surprise:
besides a pleasant heftiness, a sound
of sloshing can be noticed. Vapors caught
within its cooling crust were liquefied,
and linger still, a million-year-old vintage.
Although one might recall the once ubiquitous
snowstorm-in-a-glass-globe paperweights,
this offers us no view inside to gauge
the wild weather a shake or two incites.
Turbulence masked by hard opacity. ...
If we could, which would we rather see?
Age-old distillate, infant tears of the earth,
or gem-like crystal of the inner walls
harboring them like some fair reliquary?
To see the one we'd have to spill the other.
Better to keep it homely and intact,
a witness to the worth of hiddenness,
which, in regard to our own kind, we call
reticence, and in terms of higher things,
mystery. Let the elixir drench unseen
the facets that enshrine it, world without end.

CAVE

> *May it be right, and fitting, by your will,*
> *That I describe the deep world sunk in darkness*
> *Under the earth.*
>   Virgil, *Aeneid* VI, 268-270
>   (trans. Robert Fitzgerald)

The young man in his flannel shirt and khakis
brandishes no caduceus but a flashlight,
striding along in work boots with decidedly
unwinged heels, but for all that he makes
a credible enough tour guide for this
low-tech excursion down below the surface.
The way down from the entrance is a steel
ladder-like stair most people go down backwards.
Prosaic bulbs throw beams down from the roofs
of the main tunnels (our leader's blunt electric
wand is just to show up shadowed corners),
and the floor evidently is swept. Beyond that,
everything here is left almost the way
it was when the first nosy local farmer
found out what underlay his sloping pasture.
One day over a century ago
he let himself down with a rope and lantern
after he'd cleared the heap of rocks away
that hid the cave from sight but couldn't block
the cool air pushing from it, making that
a favorite spot for cows to congregate
when the whole countryside fell limp with heat.
(It was the sight of them so well-contented
that made their owner curious for the cause.)
Once down he found, as we do, sweater weather,
summer or winter, a steady 48°.

When he led tours, he'd stretch them out for hours,
providing lunches, lanterns, mackintoshes
for those who ponied up with extra fees.
We're just as glad to have a quicker, less
encumbered chthonic thrill. We'll have lunch elsewhere.

So what is there to see? As usual,
the freaks of limestone, fancifully named:
here's Pluto's Throne, Persephone's Wedding Cake.
Flowstone in rippling ridges sheathes a boulder,
mimicking a Pacific giant clam.
Continuing the marine motif, a recess
sports teeth like a shark's jaws, each incisor
adding ferocious smidgens on the way
to clamping shut some centuries from now.
Damp portions of roof let down stalactites
ranging from toothpick-size to walrus-tusk.
Some larger ones lie shattered where they fell
like toppled columns of a ruined temple.
Having been down in more spectacular caves
(the sort that one could fittingly call caverns),
I am no more than mildly diverted
by such calciferous doodads. What I follow
with more sustained attention is the stream.
At first a measly runnel to our right,
like one that snakes across my cellar floor
in time of thaw after a snowy winter,
it widens to a few feet as we walk
along its edge, the children in the party
looking excitedly for eyeless fish.
Excitedly and all in vain: we're told
the only tenants of the rivulet
anyone's ever seen are salamanders,
shy and albino, just now not in view.
You might say this is nothing much to look at,
and you'd be right. What holds me is the sound,

which seems far louder than a stream this size
would make in open air. We turn a corner,
and meet the reason: here at the back wall
the tour perforce must end at, is the water's
origin, a cataract whose lip
is inches from the ceiling, pouring down
a dozen feet to feed the course we've traced.
Somewhere (we never see it) there must be
an outlet where the stream rejoins the sun.
But here the water's plunge into itself
gleams dully from the wattage overhead,
and the good-natured flashlight flourishes
indulged in by our guide get lost in pale
wavery curtains of cold fluency.
It's a bit mesmerizing; I imagine
that if a spattered droplet were to pass
my parted lips I might forget my life
and linger here in a Lethean spell
until a thousand years had run their cycle.
We only have a few more minutes, though,
to spend here looking and, more fixedly,
listening to the narrow-channeled tumult
caroming off the rocks that cloister it.
Would anyone who listened hear a different
message in the unflagging oracle?
Possibly. I can only testify
as my own ear is given to construe
that unemotional, relentless mantra
rivers and rains send down here with their seepage,
augering out and echoing its way
through the uncharted veins of changing earth,
an endless chant: *Not yet, not yet, not yet.*

Leaving the voice to drum on in its grotto,
I turn and take away with me from here
an image of persistence rilling under

all that we face, subordinating fear
and hope alike in a long search for daylight.
Where is the spring that rises out of these
dark passages? Having come down to see
and hear these enigmatic waters, I
would like to see them mirror the tall sky
and hear what they would say then, having broken
into the boundless air and dazzlement
of a new country they themselves renew.

IN THE REAR-VIEW MIRROR

Thinking about them as you saw them last,
you see them standing there behind your back,
leaning out into the road to wave goodbye,
lingering even as growing speed and distance
diminish them until they neatly fit
head to foot in the mirror-strip you glance at.
Tiny in your lengthening wake, still waving,
they could be nameless people on a postcard,
too far away for you to make out faces.
Then, at the first turn, they're lost completely,
places taken by someone's windbreak pines,
a split-rail fence, and then, as the wheel straightens,
nothing but empty road. Ahead of you
are towns where you will never know a soul,
exits following exits you will pass
and never take, amassing a stiff toll
finally to make good on. Fortunately
you carry along with you that higher-powered
reflective instrument that you can use

no matter how far down the road you've gone
to bring them back in view as large as life,
putting yourself in the picture, too, which makes
thinking about them as you saw them lasting.

From *Solving for X* (2002)

For Timothy Steele

*Increasing with the years but still bicoastal,
our friendship has perforce been mostly postal.
Accept this parcel, bearing scraps of gray
New England weather to you in L. A.,
as well as thanks for each new poem or letter
I welcome as a nudge to make mine better.*

THE FUTURE PERFECT

It will be recognizable: your neighborhood,
with of course some of the bigger trees
gone for pulp and the more upscale houses
sporting new riot-proof fencing which
they seem hardly to need in this calm sector
whose lawns look even more vacuumed than they used to.
Only a soft whirr of electric automobiles
ruffles unburdened air. Your own house looks
about the same, except for the solar panels.
Inside, the latest occupants sit facing
the wall-size liquid crystal flat TV screen
they haggle and commune with, ordering beach towels
or stockings, or instructing their stockbrokers,
while in the kitchen dinner cooks itself.
Why marvel over windows that flip at a touch
from clear to opaque, or carpets that a lifetime
of scuffs will never stain? This all was destined,
down to the newest model ultrasound toothbrush.
Only the stubborn, ordinary ratio
of sadness to happiness seems immune to progress,
and it will take more time than even you
have at your disposal to find out why.
The same and not the same, this venue fascinates,
spiriting you through closed familiar doors
on random unremarkable evenings when
you will have been gone
for how long?—Just a bit longer than your successors
have had to make these premises their own.
However much their climate-controlled rooms
glow vibrant with halogen, they will not see you.
But they may wonder why, for no good reason,
they find their thoughts so often drawn to the past.

BACK AGAIN

The wormy apple tree
we chainsawed to a stump
is not content to be
a barren amputee.
It has produced a clump
of rank and spindly shoots,
a thicket still unthinned,
each one a witch's wand,
suggesting that the roots
regard our surgery
as one more hostile thing
to overcome in spring,
like parried blades of wind—
mischief to live beyond.

AIRS AND GRACES

All this was years ago—back in the days
of afternoon visits between ladies
with children brought along, resigned to boredom.
Her mother always stayed for a second cup;
her mother's aunt, happy to be a hostess,
kept pressing macaroons on her niece
and grand-niece (something neither of them favored).
It always seemed to be raining when they went there
and there was no dog or cat to play with.
When the women were tired of glancing sideways
to see her fidgeting or shedding crumbs,

they'd send her to the spare room to explore
the Dress-Up Box. This could be interesting
if she was in the mood for vintage glamour.

The Box was really a modest-sized tin trunk,
lined with flowered wallpaper and filled
with bits of swank from several decades back.
There were a few dresses, much too large,
trimmed with velvet and imbued with camphor.
It was the accessories she was drawn to.
There was a pair of white gloves that on her
were almost elbow-length. The missing buttons
forced her to bunch them at her wrists, so that
she looked like a Walt Disney character.
There were various paper-and-bamboo fans
with orchids and pagodas painted on them.
She fanned her face with these and made her bangs flap.
What else? A pin made of a real seashell,
a set of tortoise-shell combs, a rhinestone bracelet.
More intriguing: an oblong of black lace,
a shawl or a mantilla, that she always
spread out before her eyes while she decided
just how to drape it. Looking through its fine,
close-knotted mesh gave her a view like one
she could have got through a sooty window screen.
Two or three hats with feathers of no color
she'd ever seen on a bird sat carefully nested.

Best of all, always to be admired,
there was a brown, weaselly-looking fur piece,
that ringed her neck and dangled down her front,
the eyes studding its narrow nut of a head
inky black and hard as rock, the nose
rubbery-feeling like an old eraser.
A little chain could cinch the snout and tail
together, but the fixed jaws wouldn't bite.

There, in the little stuffy almost-attic,
trying these in their different combinations
before a mirror, practicing to be old
and regal, she could lose track of the time.
She grew oblivious to the parlor voices
talking about people she'd never known.
Finally, when her appearance satisfied her,
she paced grandly down , the funeral veil
swathing her hair, the spineless animal
bobbling to her waist. Her mother gasped
and clapped her hands. Her great-aunt smiled briefly,
then looked into her teacup. Years would pass
before the festooned girl would realize what
her hostess must have seen: her bygone self
and her dead sisters, flaunting these fine items
when they were new, and later not so new.

A FIELD OF GOLDENROD

Midas, your fabled gleaming touch
would be hard put to burnish much
that ocher crop across the road—
like an erupting mother lode,
proliferating uncontrolled
back to the treeline, solid gold.
In truth, I doubt you could enhance
one August field's extravagance
by any glitter you could lend.
This is the wealth of summer's end;

an alchemy within the weed
will flaunt itself and scatter seed,
and summer, in a mood to splurge,
will outdo any thaumaturge.

ANTHOLOGY PIECE

Why, I sometimes wonder, out of all
the spirited conceptions of my Maker,
am I the chosen one? Reprinted ceaselessly,
misprinted sometimes (I have had death appear
in place of dearth, and yes, there is a difference),
memorized by the multitude—why me?
Something in my unmistakable rhythm
seems to have taken readers by the ear;
or could it be my undemanding scenery,
dusty road pointing ahead to sunset?
Woven snugly together with accustomed
sentiments toward all that's transitory …
What could be simpler? By this time I might
be sick of it myself, were I not bound
to bless my access to eternity.
As for the man who set my sky ablaze,
he grew to loathe my popular appeal,
but of course wasn't able to disown me.
Once I was plumper: seven lines, some good,
didn't survive the last slash of his pen.
(You'd never know: he didn't save the drafts.)
Now I am all that keeps his name alive,

pressed by hundreds of pages front and back.
Saffron pyres flicker on my horizon.
He'd have pissed on the embers if he could.

THE END OF THE SONNET

A word was missing from his fourteenth line.
He mused on how much easier it would be
if one could still wedge an apostrophe
in "over," or if cattle still were kine,
when he was yanked away from his design:
his daughter's kitten, too far up a tree,
had to be rescued. Undelightedly
he undertook to grapple with white pine,
up in whose jutting plumes of needles clung
that tiny fright incarnate and enfurred.
He got it down. His daughter's satisfaction
was ample, quick, and real. His forearm stung
with scratches, but his brain hummed with a word
found on a high branch, fathered by distraction.

DEC. 23

He's finished tacking up the Christmas garland
so it arrays the Parish Hall at one end,
loops of glistening tinsel off a rafter.

Nagged by Sunday School teachers, none of whom
could reach to do it, he brought up his ladder
and hammered through their bicker of suggestions
to pin the swags the way he damn well wanted.
Under this job tomorrow an eight-year-old
boy, a seven-year-old girl will cradle
a large, diapered baby doll between them,
while shepherds of the same age, some of them
notorious brats, stand burlap-clad with canes,
lording it over younger ones on all fours
and wrapped in artificial fleece, no lines
to learn, just lots of docile, brutish kneeling.
It's like this every year, the eve of the Eve;
hung up, the silvery furbelow now seems
to emphasize the emptiness of the space
beneath it, wintry Bethlehem of worn
linoleum facing ranks of metal chairs
he set up once the ladies left him to it.
It will have to do. Only the garland
and the direction of the gathered chairs
will make this patch of floor into a stage.
Parents, onlookers will watch as children
pretend to be parents and onlookers
in a receding time, a distant place.
Tired, he folds his ladder, bumps it down
to stow it in the basement, takes a look
at the oil burner, hearing once again
that ticking sound he doesn't like. Upstairs,
although he never aimed to make a still life,
he's done just that in absentmindedness
on a west windowsill. But no one's here
(is it too early or is it too late?)
to watch the things glint when the white spear
of sunlight touches them: his laid-aside
claw hammer and a handful of long nails.
Instruments of the Passion. Tools of somebody's trade.

THE DEVIL'S GARDEN

Just how many geological sites
or isolated rocky oddities
has man, namer of place and thing, assigned
to the Antagonist? Not the least intending
to make an inventory, over the years
I've seen, to itemize only a few,
the jungly Florida sinkhole that they call
The Devil's Millhopper, the stony pit
the western Scots have dubbed The Devil's Washtub,
and near to here, on the next mountainside,
the globed "erratic boulder"—glacial litter—
locally known to be The Devil's Punchbowl.
None of them was especially terrifying.
Nor is this—but it can seem uncanny.
Halfway up the heavily wooded side
of this untaxing mountain, suddenly
growth ceases, yields to a broad tract
of barrenness, acres of rock no pine
or birch or aspen ever grapples onto;
whatever soil once was there was ferried
down out of sight in centuries of rains.
Naturally, no trees will mean no birds.
You find yourself humming to break the silence.
This is the landscape flayed, a gaunt substratum:
if not the bowels, the gallstones of the earth.
If the rocks weren't so smooth they might suggest
the rubble left from thunderous bombing raids,
but smooth they are, an unappealing gray,
ranging in size from cobbles down to scree.
And this is what they call The Devil's Garden.

Garden no sower's hand has blessed with seed,
ground that no root will get a purchase on,

heaped with the sad, unwholesome loaves that no
wheedling flattery will turn to bread …
one can appreciate the nomenclature.
The wilderness of western Massachusetts
can serve as well as any in the world
to show the sterile harvest of negation;
here is some land not good for anything
but to be daunted by, and that not often.
Left to itself, it never changes much.
Look now and remark with what fine guile,
deeding such hard luck parcels to the Devil,
we situate his foothold safely distant
from where we live and work and raise our own
plenteous crops, a skill passed down to us
by the first gardener (yes, remember), Cain.

WAITING ROOM

Here's where the unwell (sometimes chaperoned,
if they are fortunate, by the as yet
unsick) take seats to have their patience honed:
finding not much in last year's magazines,
or aqua tiles to count upon the floor,
or what remains of the mind's slender means
to purchase a few moments to forget
what they are waiting out or waiting for
beyond the inner door.

THE ARBOR

Enter and find yourself enwrapped in green.
Ferns underfoot, vines walling in each side,
leaves coalescing in a roof provide
an ambience so nearly submarine
you wonder if you might have to grow gills
to stay in this domain of chlorophyll's.

After some moments, though, still breathing air
and thriving under that fine-woven shade
that lets in light only to stain it jade,
you see nestled in leaves what more is there:
grapes whose dimensions haven't yet surpassed
the size of peppercorns. They will at last,

and doff their camouflage, assuming tints
of Tyrian purple misting into ink.
Gladly to steep oneself, not just to think
but to watch thought grow ripe from greenest hints:
that is what vintage poets learned to do.
The marvel is, it might work here for you.

A ROADSIDE FLOCK

The weather vane designer's rundown shop
can stay rundown: it's hardly even seen
by those who blink in passing or who stop
to blink again amid the bossy sheen

of roosters mobbing porch and forecourt, bright
as newly minted pennies, shimmering so
that one imagines each undimmed by night,
vain that no common dawn could make him crow.

Not only roosters—there's a whale or two,
a trotting horse. But fowl predominate,
and N and S and E and W
all come beneath their sway. Their high estate,

if crowning house or barn in fact is such,
may at first give them a heraldic thrill.
Before we yield to envy overmuch,
let's recollect what exaltation will

commit them to: their giddy doom to pivot,
prey to the winds that flounce about the sky.
It's not the life we'd live if we could live it.
And gleam gives way to verdigris, raised high

to weather drably, exiled from the ground.
Feel that? A hint of breeze. Birds of a feather,
their regal beaks shudder without a sound,
and all the copper flock turns tail together.

"CALLED BACK"

> —Inscription on Emily Dickinson's tombstone.

We came—a Century or so
Too late—to find you Home—
We paced your Father's House—We viewed
The Tokens that your Room

Exhibits—chief, the single Dress
Cased Head to Foot in Glass—
Demurely White and Cassock-like—
Its Buttons quaint to us—

Then went Outside—an easy Walk
To where your Kin conveyed
Your Quiet Form—whose Pilgrimage
Required their Parade—

Now we—who looked to find you Here—
Are once again reproved—
Your Granite Placard curtly hints
How far Away you've moved—

Gray Words hemmed by an Iron Fence—
Latticed—by mighty Trees—
Your Postscript to the World declares
How Potent Absence is

UP AND AWAY

The brandished mirrors of the dew
grew restive as the daylight grew;
soon winked away, the myriad gleam
regrouped in subtle plumes of steam
that were as soon removed from sight—
all of this brief as it was bright.
We felt … I wouldn't say bereft,
but certainly abruptly left.
The world, indulging in its wont,
said, "Now you see it, now you don't."

The billion drops that dazzled there,
now lusterless and lost in air—
why such a rush to rarefy
and leave the meadow drab and dry?
Why couldn't they have stayed to fling
the morning sun at everything?
But if they hadn't turned to vapor,
would I be putting this on paper?
Worn out, perhaps, by shining so,
they found as comely a way to go,
and found in airy boundlessness
a fair exchange for shimmer. Yes,
one could do worse than evanesce.

DROWNED TOWNS

For John Burt

I.

Quabbin: in the tongue of the old people,
the Nipmuc tribe, the name means "many waters."
The sound of it is somehow waterlogged,
a muffled duck call in the fading light.
It is a confluence, dammed, diked, collected,
repository of rivercourse and rainfall.
Squinted at on the Massachusetts map
it looks like a schematic buzzard hunched
on a stubby branch. It came to roost there only
half a century back. For eons earlier
three veins of the Swift River, rich in trout,
bustled and brimmed through four small valley towns
to meet below them in a broader stream.

Those four towns had never a hope of growing
after they were bypassed by the railroad.
They didn't even have a hope of staying
once they attracted thirsty Boston's eye.
Dana, Enfield, Greenwich and Prescott lie
submerged beneath four hundred billion gallons.
Their destiny presents an object lesson
in the traditional civics of the Commonwealth:
to wit, what Boston wants, it gets.
(Or gets a part of: calculations vary
how many hundred thousands of piped gallons
leak out along the way there every year.)

II.

This didn't take place overnight, of course.
For over a decade it was kicked around
the Legislature, challenged in the courts,
bruited in the press. Foresighted people
started to sell out, and the tax rolls shrank.
Nearing the end, the unwilling exodus
accelerated as the locust armies
of antique dealers and house salvagers
whiled away the weekends with their pillage.
Buildings went on the block: North Dana's school
was knocked down for $35. The Town Hall
in Enfield won the highest bid that day:
$350. (It was brick.)
Anything that wasn't bought or rustled
out of the place was bulldozed and then burned.
The inhabitants of thirty-four cemeteries
were scooped up and deported to a single
tastefully shrubbed, consolidated site,
tamped down, headstones planted in stiff new rows
with no attempt to keep the culled remains
together by town. (At this late date, new neighbors!)

Before the strenuous harvest of the dead,
before the purging of the ground by fire,
the late-to-leave performed their rituals
of severance: the Firemen's Farewell Ball
in Enfield, with its black-edged invitations,
where at the end the band played "Home, Sweet Home."
The last town meetings—see how the newspaper
posed this Selectman pointing an eraser
right at the spot—there!—on the schoolhouse globe
henceforth to be rubbed out of existence.
And the depleted, brave school graduations,

classes of children fewer than a dozen
delivering earnest speeches to their elders
on topics like "Our Debt to Civilization."
And singing: "Vesper Sparrows," "Faith of Our Fathers,"
and (for the recessional) "Auld Lang Syne."

Then the last decampments, the roads closing.
The valley scalped, burned over, deeply dredged.
The two great walls of earth and concrete mounting.

The reservoir took seven years to fill.

III.

How many displaced townsfolk through the years
have stirred in sleep, revisiting the valley,
drawn back by the irresistible dream?
— You come to the center of town on your old bicycle
finding it all at first the way it was.
But there are no people walking the streets,
rocking on porches, looking out of windows.
On the picket fence of the house you're passing
the morning glory vines have been replaced
by tendrils of some rank, unlovely weed.
There is a silty, thwarted light on everything.
Look up: the sun's a muddled, wiggling yolk;
schools of fish go flickering in and out
of the Methodist Church belfry. Out of this depth
and hideous fluidity you wrench yourself,
gasping for air, and much relieved to breathe it.
Go there, though, on a summer afternoon.
The smooth, prosaic access road that ambles
into the corner set aside for parkland
leads to no tragic vision, just a view

of water up to its trick of aping sky—
blue vying with blue, above, below.
These tidy acres now are not the haunt
of human nightmare but of serene, dreamless
species who bring a touch of nature back
to soften all the mammoth engineering,
who drink but don't unduly foul the waters.
White-tailed deer, bobcat and wild turkey
browse in the fields and roam the posted woods.
Kept clean for fifty years, the sprawling lake
can be surveyed in all its magnitude
from a brutalist granite lookout tower
topping the highest hill. From there birdwatchers
swivel and tilt binoculars to catch
glimpses of eagles soaring in lordship over
waters no man fishes in by boat.
They have done well here—golden and bald eagles.
I have watched for it, but I have never seen
what Whitman saw one day: a pair in "dalliance":
"The rushing amorous contact high in space together,
The clinching interlocking claws, a living, fierce, gyrating wheel."
I have seen only solitary wheelings,
seemingly aimless till a taloned dive
ended everything for some fish or rodent.

IV.

There is a small museum in New Salem,
up at the northern tip of the reservoir,
where you can see some remnants of what was.
Dismally cased in glass are antique buttons,
knitting needles, Grange medals, Indian arrowheads;
here's a militia drum, and someone's tuba,
a couple of woodstoves and, sitting nearby

like a surrealist pun, a stovepipe hat.
Other headgear: a Union soldier's cap,
the blue faded almost to the enemy's butternut.
There are three identical wedding dresses
worn by three nonidentical sisters.
You wonder at the sheer haphazardness
of things laid out and labeled to recall
the vanished towns—so sad a miscellany
it almost looks washed up by the rising waters.
Elderly docents, veterans of the deluge,
answer most questions vaguely, through a scrim
of chancy, rambling memory in which
some few things blink though sharply:
they all remember leaving for the last time.

It was a life; it may not have been much
of a living, judging from the ineffectual
examples here and there of local industries:
soapstone foot-warmers, Shaker-style bonnets,
and the palm-leaf fans and tablemats
that women wove as piecework in the home.
One of the few real factories specialized
in curiously segmented wooden boxes,
used to entrap and transport honeybees.
You can imagine the woeful hum you'd hear,
holding an occupied one up to your ear.
The clever, brass-hinged, combless hives
sit gaping now. The abducted swarms have flown.

V.

Old citizens, solid
householders made
evictees by virtue

of eminent domain,
those of you who linger
skirting the watershed
furnish us a spectacle
that is pious, piteous,
or simply cautionary;
whether we attend
your faltering museum tours
or pace between the serried
tablets of your forebears'
second and, with some luck,
final resting place.
In the span of a few years
you incurred the lifetime's
buffetings, sunderings
that are the lot of all,
but meted out to most of us
over a longer siege:
the wiping from the map
of time-honored ways
to get from here to there,
the forced conversion
of matter testable by touch
to memory's errant mist.
You sit, a dwindling few,
across the road from this
man-made, middle-aged lake,
hallowing your relics
of the times before the flood.
Looking at them, at you,
how can we fail to feel
tremors of intimation?—
knowing that, behind our backs,
the water is always rising.

SNOWPLOW IN THE NIGHT

The Public Works Department juggernaut
mounted its customary grand onslaught
long after I, like most, had gone to bed.
Did it affect me? No one but the dead
could sleep through diesel-powered din like that.
Implacably compelling snow to scat,
cyclopean commotion cleared the road.
And that was my first hint that it had snowed.
Spirited out of clouds to drop or swirl,
then aggregate as ermine trimmed with pearl,
these bridal trappings that were just bulldozed
made their appearance while my eyes were closed.
Now that I look, what lingers to be seen
is worlds away from anything pristine.
The poet who lamented last year's snow
might have been stunned to see this midnight's go
from gossamer to gutter-hugging mound
nearly as quickly as it kissed the ground.
Men of the plow, I missed your surging by.
Here at the window, though, I wonder why
your gritty barrows lumped along the curb
have in their heaps such power to perturb.
Looking too long at sullied residue
that lines a road that leads to nowhere new,
I think of all the things I've slumbered through.

ESPALIER

Hugging its trellis, backed by sunny bricks,
this tree will never cast a shadow. Splayed
symmetrically, arboreal crucifix,
its aim in life appears to be to trade

its three dimensions for a tidier two.
You say it makes you wince, that rigid reach
to left and right. But all that gardeners do
along these lines ensures the tender peach

firm buttressing against the wind, and sun's
largesse enlarged on a south-facing wall.
Such fruits are juicier than unfettered ones
whose laden branches splinter as they sprawl.

What am I saying? What we call a fetter
may be a means of turning green to gold.
Words, I have found, abide the seasons better
spread to the light in meter's faithful hold.

SOLVING FOR X

Protean emblem, how to pin you down?
You are the unknown quantity in hiding
behind a blackboard's haze of wasted chalk,
mark on a treasure map a second look
proves innocent of place names or of bearings,
malefactor pursued through twenty chapters

to be unmasked by equally fictitious
detectives who would miss you in real life.
Miss you—because you flourish so profusely,
straddling so many contexts (sacred, sinister,
rarefied, common): sparkling in the dome's
mosaic, you are the monogram of Christ
or instrument of Andrew's martyrdom;
or, white on black, the femurs crossed beneath
buccaneer's merry bogy. Black on yellow
warns more mildly: railroad tracks ahead.
Sign of a kiss, and multiplying sign,
Caesar's 10, illiterate signature,
teacher's mark in the margin ("wrong again").
Antepenultimate character, you abut
a forking path that leads to the alphabet's
ultimate fizzle—snore in a comic strip—
while you, in suchlike sagas, replace the eyes
of two-dimensional victims just gunned down.
Unable to take form without a pause
and lifting of the pen, are you implying
that two strokes representing different meanings
cancel each other out, or one the other?
But one stroke leaves the other standing, starts
the latest round of tic-tac-toe. We live
webbed in the world's converging decussations,
no further away than our own shoelaces,
bemused by the plasticity of signs
that after some initial idle noticings
beckon our attention from all sides:
stitch of a little girl's sampler (1850),
weave in a wicker porch chair, fingers crossed
just now for luck; and here, facing the water,
sturdy tape bracing each staring window
in the gray lull before the hurricane hits.

ANT IN AMBER

Ever since Fate's undeviating thumb
englobed this ant in aromatic gum,
eons of weighty chafing in the earth
have milled it to a bauble of some worth.
Nature expended quite some enterprise
in getting this poor sap to fossilize.
Now honey-hued, translucent, it displays
intact the forager of former days:
every last leg the little soldier needed
is here embalmed, or we might say embeaded.
Didn't the Greeks believe such beads were spawned
as tears of sunset, hardened as next day dawned?
Knowing the source (a long-gone, weeping tree)
makes this a different kind of prodigy—
a model instance, maybe of renewal—
interred as ant and disinterred as jewel.
Thus in our scale of values, though we can't
be sure it would appear so to the ant.

WISHING WELL

Incredible to calculate how many
longings amass here. Each descending penny

carries a bid for love or luck, or sunny
weekends all summer, or (imagine!) money—

all on exhibit, that abounding range

of wants caressed by ripples. Just small change,

but, as we all by now must be aware,
it's not a good investment. Fair, unfair,

mosaicing the fountain floor, the votive
offerings wink at every shallow motive

that sent them to sit quiet, soak and grow:
our copper-scaled leviathan below.

A FLASHBACK

I owe this to a twisted knee.
Limping upstairs reminded me
of early days when I would put
on the first step a cautious foot,
then draw the other up beside it.
Quicker, of course, each time I tried it,
but at its best my start-and-stop
was a slow way to reach the top.
When I got there and turned to see
the cliff I'd conquered manfully
dwindling toward a far-off floor,
I wasn't ready yet for more.
Taking the onus off my feet,
I went down tamely, on my seat.

LETTER OF RECOMMENDATION

Miss A, who graduated six years back
has air-expressed me an imposing stack
of forms in furtherance of her heart's desire:
a Ph.D. Not wishing to deny her,
I dredge around for something laudatory
to say that won't be simply a tall story;
in fact, I search for memories of her,
and draw a blank—or say, at best a blur.
Was hers the class in that ungodly room
whose creaking door slammed with a sonic boom,
whose radiators twangled for the first
ten minutes, and then hissed, and (this was worst)
subsided with a long, regretful sigh?
Yes, there, as every Wednesday we would try
to overlook cacophony and bring
our wits to bear on some distinguished thing
some poet sometime wrote, Miss A would sit
calm in a middle row and ponder it.
Blonde, I believe, and quiet (so many are).
A dutiful note-taker. Not a star.
Roundheads and Cavaliers received their due
notice from her before the term was through.
She wrote a paper on ... could it have been
"Milton's Idea of Original Sin"?
Or was it "Deathbed Imagery in Donne"?
Whichever, it was likely not much fun
for her. It wasn't bad, though I've seen better.
But I can hardly say that in a letter
like this one, now refusing to take shape
even as wispy memories escape
the reach of certitude. Try as I may,
I cannot render palpable Miss A,
who, with five hundred classmates, left few traces

when she decamped. Those mortarboard-crowned faces,
multitudes, beaming, ardent to improve
a world advancing dumbly in its groove,
crossing the stage that day—to be consigned
to a cold-storage portion of the mind …
What could be sadder? (She remembered *me*.)
The transcript says I gave Miss A a B.

OUT OF CHARACTER

The colleague almost no one else could stand—
(at meetings he would lecture the Department
on what they ought to know, i.e., what art meant),
a pest who never did a thing unplanned

or unnarrated, pompous to his peers,
inflicting monologue on the unwary
who hadn't yet learned his itinerary,
anesthetizing classes down the years,

brandishing that unfinished manuscript
decades of secretaries came to dread—
unnerved them all one day by dropping dead.
Once they allowed themselves some less tight-lipped

reactions, they agreed: the place would now
be far more livable. No more harangues,
even the tenderest sighed, and felt no pangs
till their next meeting, when they noticed how

lack of those canned digressions, even lack

of that annoying punctuating cough
threw their own pace of conversation off,
summoning their bemused attention back

to note his present absence at the table.
Could irritation be like joy or love,
something we miss, and need some quota of
to live as vividly as we are able?

MAKING DO

Who can forget the ripple of disgust
that twisted the piano tuner's lip
on viewing the repair some former owner
(oh no, not us) had made with a bootlace?
It did the job, holding the pedal up.
But who could fault his scandalized recoil?
By now we ought to be familiar with
that look of flouted, outraged expertise
surveying the offence of ignorant
contrivances, cheap shortcuts, slovenly
expedients only a manic devotee
of puttering could approve or even think of.
Just so, when we moved in, the electrician
stared at the spiderweb of circuitry
some tinkering precursor hooked on wiring
trellised the basement with. And the house painter
almost swallowed his cigarette when he saw
the alligatoring my hapless, hand-done
sanding had left sitting on the clapboards.

Inured to such embarrassments, I grant
their right to be disgruntled: well-equipped
professionals are honor bound to scorn
the botch and haste of clueless amateurs.
(Although, come to think of it, a major
part of their living comes from cleaning up
our mean shifts or mad ambitious messes.)
I envy their straight saw-cuts, their rock-steady
hands with a ruler, fully furnished toolkits,
top grade hardware, knowing just how poorly
versed and outfitted most are doomed to be.
When shall I ever use the right length nail,
or hang a picture not a smidge too high?
Don't we, most of us, mince up an onion
to take the place of seldom-bought shallots?
Children sent to school wearing knee patches
that almost matched, but didn't quite, have trudged
into adulthood, peering at the world
through glasses mended at the nose with tape.
Dumbly or spiritedly we improvise,
make do with what we have in the brief time
allotted to these tasks that from above
must look like kindergarten projects done
with sometimes careful, often clumsy fingers.
Making do, we don't always do badly.
I think of Dr. Johnson's blind housekeeper
judging the level of the tea she poured
by holding a practiced finger in the cup;
or of my Revolutionary ancestor,
doing his bit by firing his cannon
into the red lines till his powder patch
burned through, after which he used both thumbs
and several fingers. It was what he had.

PILGRIMS

White as a baby's tooth, the little church
pokes up from the apostate wilderness
of onetime farms gone back to scrubby woods.
Everything's cradled snug in sabbath peace
as we approach, but suddenly, as if
we'd tripped a wire, there is a soft moan
and wheeze set off inside—the balky organ—
and then the singing, adamant and loud,
vehement exhalations taking heart
from heaving all together, as though one
ultimate heave could raise the clapboard box
off its foundation, scooting it to heaven
on a self-generated gust of rapture.
Choir practice, probably, this being
Saturday afternoon. Pent in their resonant
unornamented boards, the choir must
comprise a great part of the congregation,
so dollhouse-like the building is. The hymn
trumpets a challenge to the tuckered-out
surrounding countryside to the effect of
Hear and be saved—which is, of course, beyond
its compass, sunk in drought-depleted stupor.
Casual, sweating passersby like us
may not intend to pay much greater heed;
but a few words do pelt us, slipping through
the chuffed accompaniment, the weighty drone.
Something about "O Savior, when we die
(de-dum, de-dum) thy dwelling place on high."
Words are prone to blur in the fervent yearning
broadcast from the louvered bottom panes
of those embattled-looking pointy windows.
Haunting the air, it cannot stir the dust
even as much as we do, shuffling past.

While we're still in earshot, the sound dies.
Rehearsal must be over. Yes, they're coming
out now, and I count them, half a dozen
women and four men. They clamber into
a decommissioned school bus, painted blue,
which we now see was parked around in back.
And we, wrapped in heat and resumed silence,
what are we out here looking for today?
We keep on going, down to the dry creek
to hunt for arrowheads. It's said to be
the place for this, but after a hot hour
of scrabbling through the pebble beds we find
exactly two, a flint for each of us.
Chipped to a razor-edge, they're tapered to
carpenter-gothic points much like the windows
out of which poured the ministry of song.
Which are the points that nick the soul more keenly—
those of the lost or those of the lingering tribe?

OTHER EYES

Potato's

This tuber's dark protuberance aches to be
above ground, where there's so much more to see,

but lacking claws to scrabble like a mole
its tunnel upward to an exit hole,

it gambles all on its remaining hope—
the sprout it nudges up, the periscope.

Peacock's

The evil eye, enshrined and multiplied,
fanned out and flaunted in the strut of pride?

Fatuous folklore. Such eyes by the tailful
worship the sun, exuding nothing baleful,

offering tribute with their iridescence.
Only on us has pride bestowed its essence.

Hurricane's

Everything has a center. This is yours:
here, after all those savage slamming doors,

your inner sanctum of dumbfounding quiet,
turning a blind eye to winds at riot.

Seeing's believing. Glimpsing void, we guess
that mayhem is a mask for emptiness.

Daisy

Not often now in flower or in word
is *day's eye* even dimly seen or heard.

Our Anglo-Saxon's rusty. But the gaze
that suddenly meets ours on sunny days

can still remind us: little drop of sun
staring from petals, metaphor not done.

QWERTY

The quick red fox our fingers trained to jump
over the lazy brown dogs so that we
could tell our keys were working properly
has come to a full stop. His russet rump,

that levitated on so many pages,
can loll at ease, ringed by his treasured tail.
Now on his own, he leaves no paper trail,
and though his years of service brought no wages

our kind neglect should let him rest unseen
and unmolested, thanks to this refinement—
no need to test these pixels for alignment.
Could he be lurking, though, behind the screen,

unready for a life unmonitored,
yellow eyes puzzled, wanting to know why
we'd let him, like those logy canines, lie?
Hunters of words, we roused him with a word;

quick on the jump but not quick to forget,
his ears are pricked for the old click-and-clack
that called him periodically back
to scramble madly through the alphabet.

A DRAINED FOUNTAIN

This nameless naiad hasn't got a prayer
of filling the wide bowl her stepping stool
stands in the middle of, a granite stilt.
Blind to the disappearance of her pool,
holding an urn still at a lavish tilt,
she perseveres, pouring air into air.

A bird, inquisitive, who wet his wings
daily in ripples brimming at her feet,
lights on her earnest, weatherbeaten head
but soon departs to find a cheerier seat.
The backdrop trees will jettison their dead
to line this basin once alive with springs

sooner than not—the nights are that much colder.
Nothing can faze this maiden, though. Her poise,
braving the halt imposed on her cascade,
can almost conjure back its pattering noise,
its rainbow glints. She labors undismayed,
and if it's labor lost, nobody's told her.

From *Aromatics* (2011)

For Rachel Hadas

Bad times give way to worse.
Whatever blight's in style,
we cling to thinking verse
is something worth our while.

In these dejected days,
some lines I linger on
are yours, drawn from the maze
surrounding Helicon.

The zodiac revolves.
But words in firm array
outwear what time dissolves,
say what we live to say.

WILD TURKEYS

Out of the woods and into the side yard
they come in a slow march, a band of three,
dowdy, diagonal in somber plumes
that so englobe their awkward, ambling bodies
it is hard to believe their pipestem legs
truly support them as they promenade.
Their raw red necks and bare heads—slaty blue—
go with the legs, austere, deliberate, wiry,
seconding every step with a prim nod,
while now and then pausing to stoop and nip
whatever seeds or beetles their bead-eyes
have got a bead on. When they reach the foot
of the hill they advance gamely, helping themselves
with little hops and only a faint stirring
of wings, going up with uncanny lightness,
almost as though inflated (which in a sense
they are, given the air caught up inside
their fusty basketry of quills and pinions).
Whether on forage or reconnaissance,
they know where they are going with no hustle;
they are as much unwavering as wild.
Soon they pace out of sight, three emissaries
of shadow taking time to appraise sunshine
on a warm day two weeks before Thanksgiving,
intent as Pilgrims turning out for a hanging.

THE ODOMETER

It was long ago, in the days before seatbelts.
They were all jammed into their secondhand Chrysler,
      three children rumpusing in back,
their zookeepers up front, off to the store

on a hot summer Saturday, when the driver
noticed that something mildly educational
      was about to occur before
their eyes, if they would all pipe down and pin

said eyes to the dashboard. On it, the mileage glowed
faintly at 99,999. In a minute
      they would see a Hundred Thousand
announce itself. The children held their breath.

And then the dénouement: no more room on the gauge,
so what came gliding up was not the number they
      had fizzing in their minds. Instead:
zero, zero, zero, zero, zero.

After a second of befuddlement, the two
older brothers giggled and yelled, "The car is new!"
      The youngest sat back scornfully.
No matter what they said, he knew it wasn't.

He was right: their traveling ambience altered
not a jot. The worn upholstery's dust-imbued,
      dry-roasted smell, the pennies lost
down cracks with stray gum wrappers—all stayed put.

Up front, gripping the wheel a little tighter, their
father thought, *Another couple thousand, and*
      this heap gets traded. Their mother

felt rather than thought, *Some things go too far*

to think about starting over again, and soon
nobody noticed the no-longer magical
        numbers running, the children now
muffled by a candybar split three ways.

AROMATICS

I.

The candle factory's display room runs
about the length of half a football field.
Under its warehouse trussing and the hard
fluorescence pouring down, the aisles teem
with candle mavens bending over bins.
Hanging from crook'd elbows are the baskets
that might once have cradled new-laid eggs;
here, each one is soon lined with a stash
of pick-your-own assortment votive charmers.
Color-coded roughly along a spectrum—
at one end white, the other black, and in
between, three milling aisles of wax rainbow—
the nubbins nestle like the tips of crayons
destined for giant children, though the wicks
tufting them plainly indicate their function,
and reconfirm them as a fireman's nightmare.

Candles—in this enlightened age, who needs them?
Everyone and his mother, it appears.
And what they're after more than anything

is opportunity to choose aromas.
Only their free-range sniffing can determine
which of these mood-enhancers match their craving,
and which of them are not worth sniffing at.
For each person bee-lining it to Balsam
or Bayberry (stick-in-the-mud scents),
ten are smitten with selections named
like plein-air studies by Impressionists:
Nantucket Noon, Spring Showers, Mountain Meadow.
Others make one think of dessert menus:
Spiced Apple, Chocolate Cupcake, Key Lime Pie.
Each item offers its particular
sensation, more or less in keeping with
its label's promise. Harder to describe
is the effect of all these scents combining,
making a nectared atmosphere so dense
that one looks up expecting to see clouds
of some uncannily perfumed miasma.
Five parts myrrh to four parts bubblegum?
But that's not really it: the odor's so
composite, swaddling, and synthesized
it leaves the ordinary nose confounded.
Stepping out into the open air,
one needs a moment to recover what
the rank world habitually smells like:
sun-beaten asphalt, parking-lot exhaust,
a big dog trotting past who needs a bath.

II.

Sensory overload can be a more
decorous and exclusive exercise.
Recall the Meiji era's "incense parties"
mistily but evocatively sketched

by Lafcadio Hearn in a choice chapter
(see *In Ghostly Japan*). Envision each
kimonoed esthete bowing toward the censer,
essaying to identify each scent
with an allotted set of inhalations.
Imagine what a pungent satisfaction
it must have been to rightly tell apart
Plum Flower's wraith from that of Evening Dusk
or Dew-on-the-Mountain-Path. At intervals,
to reawaken numbed olfactory nerves,
the guests would rinse their mouths with vinegar.

III.

Much of a muchness … odorous bombardment,
whether democratized or rarefied,
leaves us at length unable to sort out
what we are smelling, or remember it.
It's the less pressing attars that impress.
In the net-curtained house of childhood,
Grandmother's alabaster jar once sat,
its lid cracked and providently mended,
waiting for your inspection. Carefully
(and furtively, now knowing how the lid
behaved when dropped), you uncovered the trove
of vintage, forty-year-old potpourri.
The hoarded petals long had lost their blush;
they might have been tobacco shreds to look at.
But there was still—amazingly—a fragrance
kept for a child's nostrils to ensnare,
the ghost of a ghost of a rose upon the brink
of utter vanishment into the dull
air of the front parlor. You could sense it
smoldering in the heatless fire of time,

each time fainter yet never fully spent—
an emanation now in its way still there
years after your last clandestine tryst,
wisping up when memory lifts the lid.

TANTALUS

The water, pure as any in a dream,
lapping his legs, the plump and purple fruit
tugging the bough down close enough for him
to smell the ripeness—these were practiced props.
They carried out their orders to the letter,
fleeing his reach of hunger or of thirst
as quickly as his muscles tensed and twitched,
as absolutely as his need struck home.
After the first couple of thousand years
it was predictable. Something less predictable
happened over the next few thousand to
his attitude (and this was very strange,
for isn't life eternal said to be
immutable?). So subtly it occurred,
he scarcely gauged the change but only knew
one day he didn't want them any more,
wouldn't have sunk his teeth into that plum
or guzzled down that teasing rivulet
for anything that anyone could pay him.
But he could never bring himself to act
accordingly, to own up to indifference.
Odd that desire's end should foster shame.
It was still punishment, but of an altered
character, to watch the dodgy, now-

no-longer-tantalizing imps of appetite
playing their part as he in turn played his,
leaning to grab at that recycled fare
whose grip on his awareness still persisted
centuries after the last pang truly gnawed.
How else now could he live up to his name?

A NEW LIFE

Everyone knows the story. Just when I thought
I was lost, a kindlier fate intervened,
rooted me to the cool ground, a mockery
to the god burning after me, whose fingers
finally lighted on bark instead of flesh.
In no time, it seemed, I grew to be at peace
with the change, and perhaps that was the reason:
this was nothing like time as I had known it,
only an unhurried, tranquil rotation
to whose unthreatening rhythm all my leaves
responded, flourished, gave way, and were replaced.
What no one seems to know is that this idyll
came to an end with just as little warning
as when it started. I have lately wondered
if what happened was triggered by the eclipse.
It was when the midday birds, bewildered, sang
their go-to-bed song that I began to feel
seized everywhere by alarm as nerves awoke
to rattle again their chains of coded sparks.
My sweet sap turned to salt, to the old flavor
of blood and tears. I looked in the old way then
(that is, through tears) to see my earlier form

emerging vulnerable and pallid from
the sheath of bark disintegrating round it.
Once again I was cornered into trading
one set of limbs for another. My hair fell
dense to my shoulders, too heavy to be stirred
by random winds to which my leaves had whispered.
My single tongue hid in my mouth, a stunned lump
incapable as yet of utterance. Still,
none of this could surpass the punishing shock
of my first steps away from stasis: crossing
the mossy turf was like walking on ground glass.

The world's pain was a thing I had forgotten.
I admit, with time (with one step at a time),
I grew accustomed to the new state of things.
The sun slid out from behind the shadow, but
paid no attention as I set out in search
of what I had done without for years, a roof.
It seems that one can get used to anything,
given enough time and a lack of options.
It may be true that every mode of being
offers advantages. Oh, but this new life
of mine would rest more easily on me if
I could forget those seasons that I spent
standing in one spot under the changing sky,
living without expectancy or effort.

THE BETTER PART OF VALOR

A would-be body surfer, eight years old,
he fell in with the ocean's mood of calm,

reviewing each low swell as it unrolled
before him its obsequious salaam.

Crossing the fringe of foam with splashing stride,
he found himself knee-deep, waist-deep, and still
nothing swung by worth joining for a ride.
Level and lazy lay the sea. Until

the chastening wave upreared a glassy face,
its towering onset tugging up his eyes
to see it beetling. He was locked in place,
discovering how doom can paralyze.

Punitive pounding, surging overthrow,
churning immersion, brackish aftermath,
it was embarrassing to undergo.
The water was as placid as a bath

after this one leviathan hit land,
leaving him for a time to drip and look
daggers at where he'd been from safe on sand.
It was the oldest lesson in the book

that sank in as he sniffled, nursed a scrape,
and kept his jarred attention on the matter.
He would become a master of escape:
when offered fight or flight he'd pick the latter.

Having survived the deluge, common sense
would hold him back from an unequal brawl
with such a mass of green malevolence
a billion times his age and twice as tall.

Deciding this revived his dampened spirit
somewhat. But as long as he would live,

he'd rate the way it hid till he came near it
with things too deep to fathom or forgive.

IRIDESCENCE

Coming and going on the pigeon's
violet throat, a flash of aqua
each time it dipped or twisted, much like
colors she saw spawned in soap bubbles
under the sun in the draining sink:
those were sights she hoarded, along with
the oil-spill on the rain-dark asphalt,
a shifting bull's-eye target of gold
and green with a wider band of mauve.
Clearly (and as her mother told her)
she needed more to do with herself.

Summer was long, and not much happened
when you were ten. Between marriages,
her mother had a certain amount
of "social life" to which she was not
a party. When she recalled that time
she never pictured her mother dressed
for work, but wearing what she thought of
as "the rainbow blouse"—it must have been
shot silk or something, the way it veered
from ripples of pink to stormy blue.
It looked terrific on her, and that
might have been reason enough to gel
that memory of it. Something more
attached to this, though: on one of those

boring Sundays when she got up late,
she found her mother in the kitchen
after a night out with Mr. X,
still, surprisingly, with the blouse on,
nursing a cooled-off cup of coffee.
Something was off-key. She looked again.
What at first she'd seen as eye-shadow
was a dramatically contused
right eye, a shiner just as vivid
as the prized oil-slick on the driveway.
It was frightening because it was
not entirely unbeautiful.
"What did that?" she breathed. After a gap
the answer: "I ran into a door."
And the door shut on further questions,
then or ever. She remembered, though,
how, as if tinged by the deepening
of her unsettlement, the beaming
day flickered into something darker.

BUTTERFLY AT THE BEACH

Between the swell of dune and swell of tide
the scene's predictable: the wet and wide
horizon, each new breaker's suicide,

the children building castles and the crowd
sprawling on beach towels, variously endowed,
gulls raiding trash cans, the occasional loud

plane out of nowhere. But amid all this, why,

with nodding blossoms not at all nearby,
has one quixotic saffron butterfly

come to survey the doings of the ocean?
Mesmerized by the scent of tanning lotion?
Or subject to some freak wind's random motion,

heaving it on a sojourn over sand?
Without even a beach rose close at hand,
chances of its alighting aren't so grand

unless someone's Hawaiian floral print
(though offering nothing tastier than lint)
should tempt it to inspect each raucous tint.

No caftan or bikini features quite
enough bouquet to snag its appetite.
It courses down the coastline—exit right. …

A sense that we ourselves have overstayed
drifts in. All the attention that we paid
to that unflagging aerial parade

yields to a sudden feeling that the place is
more of a desert now, less an oasis.
Fluttering fool wings brightly in our faces,

the bug betrayed no doubt where it should go.
Perhaps beyond these miles of ebb and flow
there may be flowers to feed on. Be it so.

WHAT SHE FOUND

All her life long
(and it was long)
she had a knack
for finding these:
out in the midst
of an uncut lawn,
whenever she wanted,
seemingly,
she could reach down
and deftly harvest
a four-leaf clover,
a summer trophy.
Most of her other
accomplishments
were unremarkable:
knowing the names
of birds and flowers,
making a passable
jelly or piecrust.
Maiden-aunt hobbies
made up her life.

But her reconnaissance
skills outdid us.
Nobody else
had such an eye:
cunningly camouflaged
green on green,
the lucky tokens
were safe from us.
Near to ninety,
she still could find them.

We never knew
what she did with them
until, years after
her unabrupt
but mild departure,
a cache turned up
in a garden book:
pressed between tidy
squares of wax paper,
a good half-dozen
looked up at us,
a squad of little
playing-card clubs
(but four-lobed, freakish),
their stems gone brittle,
their color changed
to the olive drab
of some old knapsack.
Veterans, back
on hand to recall
the luck that missed us
but lit upon her,
untransferable,
such as it was.

OAK LEAVES IN WINTER

The leaves that are the last to leave,
clinging to low-down limbs of oak,
would be, I think, the last to grieve
for greener days gone up in smoke.

Not much to look at, crackly, brown,
dowdy with Gothic points and curves,
durable, like the wood they crown,
they hug resilience in reserves

their more flamboyant counterparts
at the first cold let fly entire.
When the red maples hurled their darts
it was their pride to hold their fire.

Now, having shunned the fusillade
that brought their gaudier neighbors low,
they taunt the season as they fade,
defy the wind, look down on snow.

MEMORY

A book that has contrived to hide itself
from you for months turns up one afternoon
point-blank, as you reach for a nearby volume—
misshelved, of course, and who's to blame for that?
You bring it down and plant it on the table
under a decent light and open it
to where you think you'll find the passage you
were hoping for, ensconced in some eventful
middle chapter. But the spine is tight,
spring-loaded, you might think, so avidly
the pages rise whenever you lift your thumb
and flip back to the outset of the story,
determined to begin at the beginning

without which, after all, nothing makes sense.

How commonplace it grows to lose your place
when every search withers to retrospection.
There by the window glazed against a view
you know by heart and rarely choose to look at,
the fanned pages practice recalcitrance,
harking back as if they were enraptured
atavists, or as if they gave themselves
up to a breeze you can't feel on your skin.

HABIT

His hand went fishing in the silver drawer,
doing its thing with no express command,
the same as it had done the days before.
What did it know, this practiced helping hand,

ferreting after spoons and forks and knives,
gathering up its clutch of two of each?
Plant habit in the muscles and it thrives;
in absentmindedness it fills the breach.

Disquiet halted him as he was turning
to set two places. What could be the matter?
No. ... Yes. As if he'd handled something burning,
he let the flatware drop with a dull clatter,

reminded that, from now on, one place setting
would do. His hand would have to learn forgetting.

THE POE TOASTER PREPARES FOR HIS ANNUAL VISIT

The weatherman's predicting sleet tonight.
As if I needed one more disincentive ...
It was Father who was the fanatic.
His self-appointed dive into the Poe
Centennial in 1949
was such a thrill he had to re-enact it,
and did, for more than forty years. If I
should last as long I'll be amazed and grateful.
(Grateful to be alive, I mean, not grateful
to be persisting in this homemade homage.)
Father adored it all: the black fedora,
the scarf masking his face, the silver-tipped
cane he didn't need at first, then did
in his last decade. Faithful to his whim,
he'd slink out every January 19th
in the small hours, the raw Baltimore night,
and make his shadowy pilgrimage to Poe's
belated monument with its carved raven
that doesn't look much different from a seagull.
Ceremoniously he placed oblations:
cognac, a good label, the bottle partly
drained by the ritual drams he'd savored
before venturing out, and three red roses.
("Blood-red" was what the papers always said.)
Steering clear of the poor, sleep-deprived
reporters on the prowl to get a story
as spooky as they could from his routine,
he made his way back home to us, replete
with duty done, the Master's birthday marked.
Finally when it got to be too much
for him, he added to his offerings
a note, unsigned, announcing to the world:

"The torch will be passed." So, from then on, this
became my annual responsibility.

I'd like to say I felt enthusiasm,
but it was something more like resignation.
 A Presbyterian churchyard's not the most
cozy of spots in dead of night in winter;
and still, when I see "Toaster" in a headline,
"kitchen appliance" pops up in my head.
Poe, I suspect, could care less. People say
he may not even be beneath that stone,
the wrong set of bones having been moved there.
(Bodies that don't stay put: a theme of his.)
I don't care much for cognac, and in fact,
to get down to it, I can take or leave
that feverish stuff he wrote: the soggy verses,
the tales with nut-case narrators expounding,
the razor-brandishing orang-outang,
the pit—the pendulum—the walled-up cat—
and all those dashes darting round the page.
But there are always readers who succumb
to lines like "Death looks gigantically down."
(That's one that even I think not too bad.)

In any case, I'll see it through tonight.
Father's been gone some years and still it seems
I haven't got the heart to disappoint him.
Nowadays the only hint of challenge
comes in evading what's become a pack
of partyers who crowd the gates to spy
and shiver in the slush. It isn't hard, though.
They won't accost me, having no great wish
to put a mundane end to this enigma.
To them I'm something here in Baltimore
like Pennsylvania's groundhog, showing up
to do my bit dependably in public,

worth a few column inches every winter.
It adds a modicum of atmosphere,
and atmosphere was everything to Poe.
Does he look down gigantically at us?
Poe didn't live for long in Baltimore,
but he's been dead here for a long, long time.

A SPIRIT PHOTOGRAPH: W. B. YEATS AND ANOTHER

The specter, just as you'd expect, is pale—
the disembodied hovering face appears
almost as chalky (and almost as round)
as a digestive tablet, moored in air
at a sharp tilt, occluding with its haze
the right-hand swag of the poet's regal mane.
Like an invisibly tethered, murkily
lit balloon but for some key details:
lips wistfully parted, a long streak
stained dark as a silent movie star's,
and up above, nose blurred to nothing, eyes
unfocused, or (in this mercurial image)
so *out*-of-focus no intent or sentiment
declares itself in them: a pair of raisins
studding a pallid bun. Below, the poet
patiently sits, affording a distinguished
anchorage for this ethereal waif.

Behind tortoiseshell spectacles, his own
eyes are harbored so deep in their sockets
you cannot see if they are shut or staring,

aiming at inward or at outward vision.
Then too, he might be simply wincing at
a flashbulb's brilliant spasm capturing
the dead communing with the quick in this
improbable tableau. Your first response
might be to giggle (mine was) at this oracle
sedate in tweeds, providing this phantasm
a perch as it takes form out of the dark
(or one might rather say out of the darkroom).

A histrionic apothegm of his
flickers in memory—something to the effect
that there are only two things of interest
to an intelligent person: sex and the dead.
Can it be so? This wan, off-center succubus
doesn't excite much interest either way,
nor is this encounter much of a tryst
since the pair, both facing us straight on,
might even be oblivious of each other.
But they're on the same wavelength, or the same
astral current—so the bland exposure
purports to testify. Designed to prove
the living and the dead share tenancy
here on the dusty earth, preposterous
but unabashed, for all its fakery
the photo makes a viewer muse. The poet's
ache to gaze clear of the cage of bone
is palpable in this as in his art—
how ready are we now to call it moonshine?
His picture curls and yellows with the years
while verses, prompted from beyond, remain
for us to read and say by heart, restoring
his dead, shrewd, credulous voice to life.

QUESTIONS ABOUT ELIZABETH BISHOP'S CLAVICHORD

Curtly mentioned in memoirs, letters—how
can we reconstitute its image now?

Was it bedecked with marquetry,
grinning with choicest ivory,

in short, the classiest keyboard
on the Eastern seaboard?

Or was it modester, a mere
well-tempered clavier

whose charm centered alone
in a congenial tone?

(Mining another source just now, I'm told
the case's color scheme was green and gold.)

But further: what did an item like that fetch
when she ordered it from Dolmetsch?

When her nerves were taut and jangling,
did it subdue them with its twangling?

Past midnight, did she sway above its tune
while her Man-Moth flittered up, up toward the moon,

warding away malaise, alarm, fatigue
with a gavotte or gigue?

Did she ever play a prelude on it for
her mentor Marianne Moore,

or master her technique at last so well
as to regale Robert Lowell

with a Galuppian sonata
while he imbibed his vodka & Salada?

Did she play études dutifully until
fate whirled her off to sambas in Brazil?

Did she absorb a loss
when she sold it finally to Howard Moss?

(As losses go, this needn't have been bruising,
but did it help her learn the art of losing?)

What favored party did it pass to, when
HM in his turn went beyond our ken?

Just where might it reside now? In
the silence of a shadowy storage bin?

Or is it kept from such cobwebbed malingering
by some baroque fan's heavy fingering?

Distempered thus from hammering overmuch,
does it, like us, lament her lighter touch

too rare in any art this noisy while
since she departed with her pliant style,

leaving to blunter hands not only these
but her beloved ABC-clad keys,

each note there too struck silvery and sure,
so that her work, our wonder, both endure?

OLD MAN OF THE MOUNTAIN

Charisma shaped his overhanging ledge,
made him iconic, heading him toward fame.
Eons on Cannon Mountain's windy edge
earned him his name.

After untold millennia, who counts?
The bare peak was his post. He stayed to man it,
staring at air and eagles, other mounts
made too of granite:

the constant sentinel who stole the scene.
His beetling brow, his massive lantern jaw,
his knife-edge nose protruding in between
indifferently cast awe

on the first scouts who pioneered the Notch,
tiptoeing past the shade of that profile.
Then followed tourist hordes to watch him watch,
with no hint of a smile,

the forests turn to farms, the straighter road
reform the ragged, snaking Indian trail.
None of these changes seemed much to forebode
a finis to his tale,

since none could change his vigil over change.
Then, one night, a vibration broke the spell.
Loosed from his lookout, leaving it vacant, strange,
his face fell.

Loss by a landslide made a sad enough
end to the reign of this New England sphinx;

sadder, to know his pose was one great bluff
riddled with chinks.

WORKING OUT

Motivation

Mens sana in corpore sano might
be every bit as true as it is trite,
but what can spur the sedentary will
recurrently to gulp the bitter pill
of sane exertion? Doctor's orders. Fright.

Trainer

Hannah can see that I am too ethereal.
Her regimens are thoughtfully designed
to keep me focused on the raw material
that for so long had somehow slipped my mind.

Treadmill

A line from Hopkins trundles through my head:
"Generations have trod, have trod, have trod."
To keep alive I mime the trooping dead.
Ten minutes more must go to this sheer plod.

Rower

Charon, your moldy prow is faintly showing
on the horizon; in my dry-docked craft
I pull against an unseen current, knowing
there is no knowing just when you'll swing aft.

Pullups

My two arms dragging up the rest of me
are painfully apprised of gravity.

Situps

My brain says I should do five more now, but
a differing opinion fills my gut.

Bench Press

Peculiar, upward thrusting: like inverted
pushups, or attempting to get rid
of a blithe Saint Bernard. Or, disconcerted,
coaxing aloft a lowering coffin lid.

Attention-Getter

His clanking on of fifty extra pounds
is followed by a train of ardent sounds,
each beefy heave accompanied by grunts
which fail to charm us less ambitious runts.

Role Model

Past eighty-seven, at a queenly pace,
she gets her money's worth out of the place,
bestowing on each Nautilus machine,
to the mind's eye, an opalescent sheen.

Locker Room

So: am I still committed? All the more so;
what if each sinew creaks from recent strife?
A glance at this or that archaic torso
reminds me I had better change my life.

THRESHOLDS

The room was dark, too dark to see
ahead to what was wall or door.
Impeded with uncertainty,
he sought to reckon where the floor

might run (it helped to know his height).
And then he saw it, like a line
ruled low upon a blackboard: light.
A minimalist exit sign,

scant, but enough to make the scope
of his environs known to him.
Years later, when he looked for hope
to get him past a shadow's rim,

he thought of how the narrow gleam
restored dimension to the gloom,
and how like shrugging off a dream
it felt to leave that shuttered room.

HILL TOWNS IN WINTER

Then there is that portion of road that seems
a detour into the nineteenth century,
looping black and ribbony, swale at each side
packed below seasonal crust. First skirting slopes
studded with those ramshackle trunks that only
the wind bothers to fell, where snow can linger
sometimes well into spring, it veers to bisect
village centers that huddle sullen and cowed,
pistol-whipped by the weather, each stark white house
a block of ice presiding in a blank yard.
Only the shoveled footpaths reassure us
that such clumps of durance are inhabited,
since no one ever steps out to take the air

as we drive past all this en route to Pittsfield.

The life inside—is it old New England still,
hived but mildly humming in hibernation?
Soothing to imagine those households, guarded
each by a tapering frieze of icicles,
wise in the ways of waiting out the winter.
The quilt to piece, the loose chair-rung to reglue,
baked-apple-dessert smells, games of Parcheesi,
kittens chasing their tails to watch. And always
the twirl and slide of needles replicating
the pairs of mittens shedding mist by the stove.
Say it could be so, it remains beyond us.
The true pulse of each place stays boxed in clapboard,
busy with it knows what. It's wise to mind
our own business, forgo time-travel, and keep
our eyes on the road. Just now, rounding a tight
curve, we've almost run into an ambulance,
halted silent behind a police car, both
flashing their frantic lights in garish contrast
to that drab colonial they have stopped at.
Though still no human figure enters the scene
in the combustive moment of our passing,
here's a reminder—by no means a relief—
that something, yes, is happening there inside,
while the gray uprush from the central chimney
(the last thing we see as the road rises)
signals nothing, and signals it to no one.

PARABLE OF THE BIRDS

They might be swallows. Barely to be seen,
they comb through what the combine left behind,
dispersed, discreet, below the radar screen
while burnished stubble gives them grain to find;

till suddenly, as though at some behest
we cannot hear but they innately share,
they've catapulted up and coalesced
before we know it, mustered in midair

in so close-knit a flock it's more a swarm.
Swung in a cluster, seized by one intent,
they could enact how scattered inklings form
the mass and movement of an argument,

or even how a poet's hunt for words
might arouse images at ease in sky.
Too neat a likeness? Defter yet, the birds
will take their bearings, never going high,

and glide, unshackled from similitude,
down to the next field for newer gleaning.
The landscape they blend into, finding food,
is one the restless eye still raids for meaning.

ONE BLACK SQUIRREL

Skirmishing under the birdfeeder, these four
    gray squirrels are beginning to show
seasonal wear as they dredge through husk piles for
    some actual seed. The latest snow

hasn't added grace to their dispositions;
    they snatch, butt, and scuffle to survive.
A palimpsest of tramplings, of collisions,
    forms under their scrum. It seems they thrive

first by bickering, then by minding the store—
    all in all, a glum crowd to survey ...
which makes this sudden newcomer all the more
    a standout against the fretful, gray,

unchummy roughhousing of that sad quartet.
    His India-ink-steeped complexion
jolts the backbiters, leaving them "freaked with jet"
    (Milton, in another connection).

And for us, his foray's choreography,
    so sinuous we could almost clap,
makes its mark finally as calligraphy
    swirled across a broad sheet of foolscap,

all of his craft poured into each arabesque
    till his transporting runes have speeded
him to the treeline. Darting from this his desk,
    he brings to mind ours. Seen and heeded,

dashing it off so deftly and then dashing,
    he's dropped hints for one good way to write:

Firm pacing. Rapid pivots. No rehashing.
Images made fast in black and white.

RIVER AND ROAD

Four days a week and sometimes five
I take my make-my-living drive
along a road I know too well.
For several miles, parallel
to mine, a river steers its course,
moving with unassuming force,
tugging its ripple-convoy south,
aiming to catch up with its mouth.
Till at a bridge we intersect
we each, in different ways, reflect:
I mull on all I need to do
while it absorbs the local view.
Absorbs? Well, no. Its surface proffers
back every sight each instant offers.
Leaves flutter from a lowdown limb
not only near but on the brim.
Glance up or down: the doubled sky
confounds a sense of low and high.
Each cloud flotilla setting sail
rates an escort in mirrored mail;
and, in the midst of all, the sun's
photons arouse rebounding ones.

If the road tended closer in
the water might display my twin,
but ferried on by asphalt, I'm

oblivious of it for the time.
Crossing from bank to bank, I go
my way and leave it to its flow.
What comes to pass upon its face
jars not a bit the river's pace.

And this goes on for days, for years.
As though through its own mist of tears
it gives the world back with a wink.
In me, though, such impressions sink
abeyant to a rambling grotto
(Room For It All might be its motto),
waiting spellbound or simply parked
for days or decades unremarked
till, surging from the silt to break
the placid surface with their wake,
they win the notice I'd withheld
before. I let our currents meld,
returning buoyancy and sheen
to a long-disregarded scene
now entertained in full and made
part of my conscious cavalcade—
with such a feeling, maybe, as
the steady-running river has
when it arrives to meet the sea
and finds a mightier harmony.
And, so it won't drop out of sight
once more, I take my pen and write.

IN STORAGE: A CALDER CAT

Curious interlopers in our households,
they come and go. And when they go for good
the ones that oddly deigned to live with us
enter a tenth life of family legend,
or say of leitmotif, always beginning
"That was the one." That was the one who caught
a bat on the roof and brought it in the window.
That was the one who always swallowed string.
That was the one who died, sadly enough,
when a tinned ham slid off the kitchen counter.
Note how often the theme is appetite.
But this one? There's no tidbit to entice him.
Between svelte and scrawny, like some we've known,
able to appear both round and flat,
lolling with one nonchalant front paw
crossed on the other, but with ears a-cock,
the negligent peg of a tail perked up
assertively—as anyone can see,
his nose is out of joint. One is not moved
to pet that coat of what looks like scuffed umber
shoe polish rubbed over streaks and whorls
of wood graining that here stand in for stripes.
But see the eyes of this barn-timber idol.
Idol or Eye Doll? Bulging like a pair
of tethered blimps, those eyes return our stare,
triggering us to blink first, intimating
that *we* are the truant pupils come to take
instruction or correction in this sanctum
of storage cabinets, the inmost shrine.
Fresh from this pilgrimage, I'd recommend
this cat stay in the cupboard. He's not one
we can imagine willing to adopt us.
Homely, heraldic, too sedate to spit,

this wooden totem's scorn for us is total.
This is the one we wince to think of, watching
even after the metal door swings shut.

THIRST AT MIDNIGHT

Looking through the skylight
a moment after midnight,
I found my gaze returned.
The seven bright eyes burned
with neither love nor hate.
Aloof, they constellate
in what we choose to call
the Dipper (Big, not small).
It seemed in line with why
I'd gotten up—mouth dry—
but I would get no sips
from its galactic dips.
We know now that the stars
can't succor human scars,
can't (in this case) fill up
a single bathroom cup.
We know, we know, we know.
Why did I linger so,
in search of something there
behind the white-hot stare?
Did I expect a drop
of nectar from up top
to trickle down and spike, or
transmute my blood to ichor?
How many kinds of thirst

had I in darkness nursed?

Scuffing a loose slipper,
I stared back at the Dipper—
too long. Then gripped the sink
and got myself a drink.

A CERTAIN OTHER SLANT

It's funny the way we say it's time to unbend
when we mean bend: dismiss the parade-ground posture,
lean with the way of the world this easy morning.
See the blinds partly askew, parsing the sun-flood
into a radiant sheaf of diagonals,
combing the bedroom rug with rich obliquity.
Where would we be without the earth's reliable
tilt that summons up summer? We should welcome it,
remembering all the gentle green gradations
leading here and beyond that give the long shadow
of the most upright tree a hammock to sag on.

Beautiful the pitch of our roof, lightly steaming
as dew takes its leave by a throng of unmapped paths.
Beautiful the moist grass, pliant beneath each breeze.
Beautiful the slope of the horse's tousled neck
as he champs his own grass in the field down the road.
But why go even that far to scout out angles?
Beautiful, just now, your inclination toward me.

SUNDIAL IN THE RAIN

Patiently waiting for the sun to rise,
the dial seems more dutiful than wise:
the sun, already up for hours, seems
a shrouded moon, so muted are its beams.
Mist complicates to drizzle, then to drops.
Like one of Thomas Hardy's dismal props,
demure atop its neo-Gothic column,
the timepiece tenders us that old unsolemn
advisory: it counts only sunny hours.
If one subtracts for night, for clouds, for showers,
that hardly makes a taxing regimen.
Always willing to work, of course, but when
is not for it or us to specify,
much as we might prefer to clear the sky.

The gnomon, less a pointer than a nose
of stiff wrought iron, juts aloft and shows
there isn't anything to do but wait,
unless to smell dank earth and meditate
on times we're just as willing not to mark.
Could we surrender to the larger dark
the shadows that our memories renew,
it would be no great trick to share the view
that keeps the dial jovially on track.
It never forfeits time in looking back,
endures inertia while the meddling storm
denies it freedom to project its form,
and holding its potential in good stead
resumes its reach as quick as light is shed.

BLUE PERIOD SKETCH

Stepping outside for once without my key,
I heard the latch click like fatality.
I felt my pockets, called myself a name
(there being no one else around to blame),
tried other doors (although I knew them locked,
leaving me self-excluded, self-bemocked).
I felt like someone's dog or cat, whose only
way to get in is to sit looking lonely
until the door mysteriously swings wide
enough to let him hustle back inside.
I pulled some weeds, then settled on a bench,
waiting to feel my wound-up nerves unclench,
and having given vent to irritation,
warily lent myself to rustication.

Well, as we all know, nothing happens when
we're on the lookout for it. Nothing then
occurred that I could not have seen if I
had chosen any day to play the spy,
guarding the garden like a sentient gnome,
familiarly displaced, strangely at home.
A pair of crows, disputing territory,
shouted out insults, grim and minatory.
A meditative cloud dispensing shade
at the yard's far end curbed its promenade
and hung at rest in a breath-catching hover.
The neighbor's cat, disgruntled to discover
a witness to his trespass, crossed the lawn,
oozed through a row of cypress and was gone.
I looked back at the sky. The cloud had drifted
after all, while my gaze had dropped and shifted.
And there it was, the sky my childhood knew.
Unbounded, elevated depths of blue

into which, lying flat on grass, I'd stare
and find no end to openness up there—
so deep a reach of blue I thought the sky's
immensity might overfill my eyes,
adding its essence to their film of tears.
I hadn't seen it quite that way for years.

For an arrested moment, though, I did.
And if the eye by lowering its lid
could hold a sight forever, I would still
be hypnotized, surveying heaven's sill.
I would be still upheld in strange rapport
with cloudless calm last seen so long before.
Its vibrancy was something elemental
(or, this being New England, transcendental).

I lost it, though, the instant that I blinked.
My grasp of it grew somehow less distinct;
the present slid uncoupled from the past;
the moment, like all moments, couldn't last.
However close we'd seemed to interfusion,
the sky and I, it was the same illusion
I had let go of, or been let go by
once days were gone when I had time for sky.
The blue withdrew itself, intact, unfading,
even as I felt drained of its pervading.
What had I wanted it to do? Imbue me,
spreading its otherworldly tint all through me?
(*Beneath* the skin—if topically bestowed,
I'd stand out, like a druid daubed with woad.)
A chasm that had narrowed to a crack
had yawned again. My separateness was back.
Communion decomposing, I was left
with one more way in which to feel bereft;
so I was more than ready when my wife
restored me to the round of daily life

by coming home and lending me her key
while trying not to laugh too much at me.

DUSK

Although the child knew the grown-up word
was not the same as *dust*, as dark invaded,
she thought of something dust-like when she heard
the old poetic term. When daylight faded,

what she believed appeared there was a host
of milling motes intent to occupy,
from ground to zenith and from coast to coast,
the ambient air and all the loftier sky—

each monad too diminutive to see
singly, of course, but in the aggregate
composing darkness as it grew to be
the ruling power after sun had set.

Not a particularly (or partic-
ulately) pleasant way for night to form.
Fortunately, the vision didn't stick.
As years went by, she blinked away the swarm.

She pays less notice now when evening falls.
Dawn is what draws her; someday she may trust
its pantomime of what an old prayer calls
the radiance that lies behind our dust.

From *A Late Spring, and After* (2016)

For Hilary

*At first I thought to say "in memory,"
but the words feel inert for what I feel.
Even at rest you go the rounds with me.
You are the steadfast axle, I the wheel.*

I. *VESSEL*

MY FIRST ATLAS

was not a book but a lamp,
a night light with attitude,
centered on the hall table
in the first house I lived in.
There, in my grandparents' manse
I stood eye-level with this
half-squatting roustabout, this
hood who looked a good deal like
a hood ornament in style.
Musclebound, with a finish
mimicking bronze, he no doubt
was pot metal through and through.

None of this mattered as much
as what the small weightlifter
was charged to keep supported
with straining arms and shoulders:
a glass globe, so much bigger
than any part of his bulk.
Only alight at night time
or on a dark afternoon,
its will-o'-the-wispish glow
wasn't one you could read by:
it kept you from stubbing your toe.
The glass had little color
until the fifteen-watt bulb
inside it flickered to life:
then it appeared as green as

a honeydew melon's flesh.
Strange molded patterns on it
probably mapped the heavens
legend asserts he upholds,
and must, to the end of time.

Next door to this, on Sundays
in his church my grandfather
held up Heaven as a thing
that sensible people should
remember to aspire to.
At night, when the other lights
were out, the glow from the hall
was just enough to lead one
to the foot of the first flight
of stairs that climbed and twisted
up into quiet darkness.

Where could the eight-inch giant
have gone to? Perhaps the glass
got broken, or someone thought
he wasn't worth rewiring.
Now in the back of my mind
he turns out to be more than
just one kind of an atlas.
He helps me find a route back.
His green light tells me to go
past him again into rooms
where all the past lies asleep.

CRAQUELURE

The ancestors were more relaxed than some
when sitting for their portraits, given that
the painter was their son, presumably
performing gratis. In their Sunday best,
they peer shrewdly from their his-and-her
twin ovals now exactly as they've done
for something like a century-and-a-half.
His formal white cravat, the filmy bands
depending from her lace cap set off healthy
complexions, features glowing with composure,
hair brushed to a sheen; in short, the earmarks
of prosperous middle age. A bead of white
glimmering from each pupil works to bring
their eyes to life. When I first pondered them,
flanking my grandparents' fireplace,
they did not seem approachable by children—
too venerable, even though their brows
were mostly free of wrinkles. Now I find
I've not only approached them but outpaced them,
drawn past their age that day they gave their son
his chance to practice on familiar subjects.

Immunity to mutability
confers on anyone a great advantage,
and for years I credited them with it.
Their sameness cast a spell of reassurance
on any of the parlors they were hung in.
Children of the latest generation
have had their turn of being sobered by them,
subdued to order by their steady gaze.
Lately, though, by sidling close enough
to give them a more skeptical inspection,
I've seen what doesn't show up from a distance:

clinging to each unworried face a wealth
of radiating fissures forming nets
of lines as delicate as hairs that once
were snugged together on the artist's brush-tip,
the one he favored for his finest strokes
to show posterity his parents' eyebrows.
Imagine filaments as fine as those,
spreading a weft, on each a weightless veil,
as if to compensate, year after year,
for all the wrinkles that would never show
in either likeness anchored to its canvas.
An aging in the surface of the paint
or in the once-protective coat of varnish
belies their images' arrested aging.

By now I'm used to this, but at the moment
it first came home to me, I thought of times
I'd made my way with care across a sheet
of pond ice till the cracks began to fan
out from my feet, warning me to back off.
Thank you, great, great Grandmother and Grandfather,
for offering a modicum of caution
along with your unruffled optimism.
No doubt you found this out before I did:
sooner or later, cracks are bound to come,
however safe our customary frames
prompt us to feel; the ice cannot be trusted
beyond a point we only recognize
on reaching it. Here, there's no turning back.

SELECTION

Matter-of-factly and midwesternly,
but with a faint shade of awe or relish,
"Struck by lightning," folks out at the farm
always got around to specifying
at times when their ill-fated former neighbor
came up in conversation. Listening,
I heard it as a single ominous word
rubbed smooth by an Ohio slur
(struckbuhlightnin). I was one of those
children with big ears, and hearing this
gave me a tingle, thinking of the reach
of savage talons ripping the night sky
we blinked at sometimes, out there in the summers.
The bone-white fire of heaven paid its visits,
so we were told, uncannily at random:
Oh, it could happen to anyone at all,
they said, caught out there under the wrong cloud.
But no, it happened to just this one they knew
(I felt like shouting, didn't even whisper),
to one they used to wave at in the field,
someone they traded tools with. That was what
struck me, not the jeopardy that reigned
aloof in cloudy generality
(by then I knew that everybody had
an expiration date); not that, but this
unshunnable, particular pinpointing
with all its mix of chance and choice for someone—
his instant, never dreamt-of claim to fame.

HANDIWORK

Against the back wall of our garage
my grandfather built a long workbench
on which whatever else we wanted
to have built for us would assume form
beneath hands that knew the ways of wood—
which meant his, plainly. My left-handed
father had no knack for carpentry,
no liking, either, but was more than
willing if the old man had a mind
to put tools smartly through their paces.
Coffee tables, cupboard shelves and doors,
bookcases, trellises and easels,
more and less structural joinery
filled his hours when he visited.
He let me heft with my untutored
hands the implements that in his hands
were like deft bodily extensions.
The handles I liked most to handle
looked like lemon jelly petrified.
Even now I have a mental grasp
of gear going about its business
capably or hung ready to hand
on hooks, or stowed on shelves: the sharp ones
he warned me about (planes, chisels, saws),
the three hammers (tack, claw, and ball-peen);
screwdrivers and wrenches in their ranked
sizes, and the spirit level with
its bubble that would never tell a lie.
Most of all I liked (I wonder why)
the pencil that he marked lumber with.
Flat, unfaceted, so it would not
roll out of sight or onto the floor,
its wooden shaft glowed tomato red.

He scored a dark line to guide his saw;
on each graphite track the saw bit down.
Sawdust from his cuts gleamed in sun-pools,
spilling down like sand in an hourglass.
Unhurried, he paid no heed to time,
had for company his tuneless hum.

If I had that pencil in my hand,
could I draw with it a straight, true line
from where I am back to where we were?
Dream on: too much has been put away
beyond the reach of recollecting hands.
Just so, he made things neat, still humming,
when a day's work was done.

                              When he died
the tools were orphaned, shunted into
an uneasy afterlife of scant
use and little skill. My parents moved;
the workbench, being built-in, stayed put
in the vacant, swept garage, its bulk
filling up the far end, standing bare
like a deconsecrated altar.

WEAR

Day after day after day,
when he sat down or stood up,
my father grabbed the arm-ends
of the captain's chair reserved
for him at the table's head.

His daily use over time
darkened the arms' finish,
leaving, as even a clean
hand will, anointings of sweat
and what else skin deposits.
A tinge, dark as from seepage
not of sweat but of shadow,
lent character to varnish,
a personal brand, compiled
of manual residue.

The antique dealers call this
"patterns of wear." Probably
the rest of us would call it
something less grand, like "grunge."
No matter what we call it,
his mark is there to behold
long after the wear and tear
he lived with day after day
increased its hold upon him
until it left him for good.
I saw how it marked his life,
but still, for the life of me,
can't see in it a pattern—
meaning, a key to explain
just where it was things went wrong.
I need to keep looking, though,
unable to set it aside,
gripped by traces of his grip
and the darker marks unseen.

A BEACON

My father used to sit on summer evenings
on the terrace until well after dark fell,
smoking with his ashtray handy beside him
on a small redwood table that *his* father
had fashioned years back from his joiner's knowhow.
If you were outside, as I would be sometimes,
turning the hose off or padlocking the shed,
you could look toward the house and see him stationed,
or rather, just discern him draped in shadow,
making himself evident by inhaling,
rousing an ember-dot of hot vermillion,
as if his cigarette end took a cue from
fireflies glimmering in and above the grass,
but unlike them, finding no answering flash.

Somewhere I must still have his cigarette case,
a dressy thing he didn't for the most part
bother to use. I haven't used it either,
feeling it his, as shown by his initials.
Thinking about him sitting in the cooling,
deepening dark, I wish I had more often
sat down beside him so we could have traded
some comfortable words before the transient,
breathtaking bits of glow ended up in ash.

THE CUSTODY OF THE EYES

His mother always told him not to stare
at people of the kind that children stare at,
people she may have thought he'd take a scare at,
out on display, it could be anywhere:

in stores, on sidewalks, lounging in the park,
missing an arm or leg that they were born with,
or more than one; or loudly trading scorn with
invisible enemies; or with eyes struck dark

staring themselves, sitting and selling matches.
He was a pliant child, and obeyed,
as wonder kindled (he was not afraid,
looking in only surreptitious snatches).

He wondered still, years on, why such protection
was furnished him. Or was it just another
lesson in better manners from his mother?
It didn't feel like that. It was projection,

he came at length to think, of her own fears
that all the rotten luck that life is host to
might possibly infect those she was close to.
A shame she never learned over the years,

as her own share of damages amassed
to prey on her and those for whom she worried,
that it was wasted effort to have hurried
her child along as she marched blinkered past,

that eyes averted make no one immune
to ambushes like those she spent life fearing.

Pulled past by her, he couldn't keep from hearing
the match seller humming a happy tune.

CÉZANNE: "THE HOUSE WITH THE CRACKED WALLS"

Jutting up from the brow of the stony hill
   presiding halfheartedly atop
a slope of green scrub and eroding boulders
   pumiced smooth like gravestones that the years
of derelict exposure have unlettered,
   this house lingers for now, evading
gravity's hunger that at a glance we know
   must have its way. Moldering yellow,
like some not-too-enticing slab of cheese,
   that wall is gouged with one off-center
erstwhile window, readier now to spill out
   darkness than let in daylight. Even
more unreassuring is the wanton crack,
   jabbing its cleavage from the faded
red-tiled roofline halfway down the languishing
   façade to where it stops like a jammed
zipper, holding in brittle check a hellbent
   cataract of yet more indwelling
darkness left by people who gave up and left.

   Why does it hurt so much to see it,
even without huffing uphill beneath that
   storm-intending sky? I never knew
the people who once lived there, never rested
   my hand on sun-warmed stucco, never

stepped around those corners into afternoon's
   east-facing shade. Yet I know the place
sufficiently to feel the wound it aches with,
   snared in its aura of destruction
just from viewing it shrunk and reproduced on
   a calendar page. A less extreme
dilapidation, I think, must be lurking
   beyond the margin as I stare at
this plight and descry, as though from the corner
   of an eye, my parents' failing porch,
sagging as time passed and incapacity,
   deepening, let it sag. That house was
white, not yellow. They moved from it years ago;
   now, side by side, they're done with moving.
And there is nothing now to be done about
   any of these things, unmendable,
except to turn the page as week follows week.

VESSEL

The imperturbability of objects:
consider, as to that, this christening bowl,
its sturdy pewter standing in for silver,
presented by my family in the mid-
nineteenth century to their creekside church—
wooden, plain, Ohio Presbyterian,
too plain, too small to need a greater font.

In 1897 that austere
edifice was torn from its foundation
when Wegee Creek, amok in a flash flood,

tumbled it downstream in several pieces.
Once the creek resumed its gravelly bed,
the bowl was found nested among some stones,
not even dented, only scratched a bit.
(Here, there seems to be a submerged theme
swirling about: sprinkling versus immersion.)
Rebuilding in a spot less near the water,
the church gave back the bowl to its presenters.
Clerical forebears on my mother's side,
first in Ohio, then in Pennsylvania,
used it to baptize the family's babies.
Perhaps it brought some luck to these occasions.

Even knowing its story, not much drama
seems to be disclosed in its design.
It has for ornament a single line
incised close to the rim, and for its base
a shallow-stepped pedestal that could rest
snugly in an officiating palm.
Grandfather, when he used it, would enhance
Philadelphia's tap water with a drop
or two of Jordan water from a bottle
some Presbyterian pilgrim had come home with.
Later, my mother kept it high and dry,
sometimes filling it with a spiky bunch
of desiccated blossoms of globe thistle—
a Scottish treatment. Since it's come to me
I've kept it empty, leaving room for thoughts.

I can't look at the sheenless color of it
without being reminded of the lowering
mass of thunderhead about to burst.
The unapologetic stern gray pewter,
mottled with age and lengthy lack of use
(no ministers of late for relatives),
looks able to withstand time's rudest inroads—

and why not? On its one foot it stood up
to water ramped in cataclysmic rage.
How soberly it wears its heritage.
Apotropaic, it outfaces storm.
Now, having been through a few storms myself,
I hold it as a token of continuance,
remembering as well that from it came,
five full decades after the flood's upheaval,
by water shed from my grandfather's fingers,
and by his saving words, my given name.

II. *NOW WE NOTICE*

DINOSAUR TRACKS

Beside the river where they used to wade
mornings or evenings in their hotter world,
relaxed as only those can be whose link
is soldered nicely high on the food chain,
they've left a mincing trail of three-toed prints
in mud that time medusa'd into slabs
of sandstone brown as mud. The steps advance,
even less hurried now than when they first
pressed muck along their marshy avenue,
then vanish where the stratum is disrupted.

Each one about a man's handspan in size
and looking avian enough to plant

visions of carnivorous prototypes
of ostriches and emus (and, in fact,
we're now informed such foragers wore feathers),
these tracks lead nowhere, and we're left to posit
the river of rivers in Connecticut
broadened and lush with swampy margins but
pursuing its primeval, silty creep
down reaches dense with hot fog and tree ferns,
as alien to us as any predator
traipsing along its banks. Again the world
is warming, sliding back toward a climate
like the one enjoyed by the old slashers,
and we, after scanning their once-soggy
plod into extinction, quicken our pace,
knowing what is forewarned and knowing too
we may at last leave less of an impression.

BELLIGERENTS

Back in the ragged woods
each crow has claimed a patch.
No changing neighborhoods
without a slanging match.

From where the pine trees tower
harsh voice and harsher voice
have jousted for an hour.
We've listened, not by choice.

Such wranglings, east or west,
are always the same story.

They need to guard the nest.
They've staked out territory.

Whose territory, though,
is what they can't agree on.
They want the world to know
they own a branch to be on,

that anyone who dares
to trespass should be wary.
This roosting place is *theirs*,
and no one else's aerie.

Just as the raucous folly
seemed bound to last till night,
it's met a check mid-volley.
Flyting gives way to flight.

The foiled conquistador
flaps somberly away;
the echoes promising gore
have nothing more to say.

The silence hovers, eerie,
until a smaller bird
peeps out a timid query
as though shy to be heard.

As featherless bystanders
we share his wonder: how
did two tough-lunged commanders
find courage to allow

their airing of aggression
room to de-escalate?
They settled for expression.

An enviable trait,

to bring an end to bluster
while it is still just noise.
If we in that passed muster
there would be fewer Troys.

"PITY THE MONSTERS!"

—Robert Lowell

Yes, at this late date, I pity them,
fang-flashers stuck in the dead-end job
of devouring bodies and / or souls
of victims hapless, foolhardy, or
corrupt, and always more on the way.
Think of Egypt's Eater of the Dead,
Ammit, equipped with crocodile head,
leopard torso, hippo hindquarters,
slumped and sulking beneath the balance
weighing the heart of each new would-be
tenant against the feather of truth.
Intent on nothing but the hoped-for
guilt overload that would fill her gorge,
she had to stay awake slavering
while Thoth droned out the court proceedings
and Anubis yawned, holding the scales.
Think of the Sphinx (the Grecian version),
part woman, part eagle, part lion,
roosting by the main road into Thebes,

a chimerical, bored toll-taker
programmed to plague each passerby
with her musty riddle, molting wings
unauthorized to flutter her off
her post even for calls of nature.
Think of the chivalry-pestered dragons
who probably wanted nothing more
than a few well-spaced human gobbets
and peace and quiet while they caressed
their coin collections, snug in their caves.
Think of the centuries of bad press,
followed by years of no one taking
them seriously—to the point that
they became moth-eaten jabberwocks
scarcely able to alarm children.
It was their misfortune that we learned,
as soon as we did, not to fear them;
and after all, why should we ever
have done so, having earlier learned
to do unto others all the things
that made them infamous—things that now
we think may remain tolerable
if kept for the most part out of sight
while we dragoon the world purged of myth
into our own brittle regimen.

THE HOUSE OF THE TRAGIC POET

would not seem all that tragic
except for our knowing it was blackened
in fuming pumice sixty feet thick,

first seared, then cooled in a petrifying bed.

      True, there are the painted walls
recycling the pathos of Troy's bitter tale.
      Bound for sacrifice, his daughter calls
to Agamemnon, whose ill-sworn vow would quail

      did he not hide his eyes, fend
away the sight of her sanctified slaughter.
      This household too lived blind to their end,
snug in their tasteful villa in this water-

      ing place of choice, adorning
the bay in view of the smoking mountain.
      Who can know what the morrow may bring,
was their art's frescoed message, and the fountain

      of blitzing ash drove it home,
obliterating their resort town idyll
      and splintering morale back in Rome.
Precious few outran the fiery overkill;

      if some from this sedate
family did, another scene they'd lived with
      might later have made them contemplate:
Helen boarding ship, embarking on her myth

      unforewarned she would return
to a dull mate's duller realm, there to remain
      a wan trophy, having seen Troy burn
to a black mound, seen her lover's army slain.

      Was she prepared to survive
the overthrow of her adopted city?
      Or did she feel, shocked to be alive,
something that scorched beyond all fear and pity?

LACHRYMATORY

Fashioned in teardrop style,
this Greek or Roman vial,

doll-sized and opaline,
like others in its line

is famed for having kept
the tears that mourners wept

processing toward the grave
of each they could not save.

They sealed their trace of salt
with loved ones in the vault.

The tribute of their tears
was meant to outlast years;

the years were meant to pass
and leave intact the glass

that held encased what grief
extorts for its relief.

This cloudy little flask
accomplished half the task,

won for its unmarred self
space on an esthete's shelf,

but let the tears take flight
sometime in the long night

before the fastened tomb
opened to air its gloom.

Now, what is here to see
is sheer metonymy—

container for contained.
If those old tears remained,

would that add emphasis?
Perhaps. But I think this

vessel enshrining void
conveys what time destroyed

far more than tears once shed
could mollify the dead.

The vacancy men face
in every time and place

it can and will express—
this dram of emptiness.

ON THE DEATH OF WILMER MILLS

This bruise discoloring my upper arm
came, as most of them do, quite by surprise,
bumping into a post or someone's elbow.
The run-in shows itself beneath the skin,
the busy lymph collected in a pond

of beige and gray, paling to feathered edges.
It pays witness to the world's buffetings,
and at a touch recalls its birth in pain.

Just so with this imponderable event.
Decades too soon, disheartening to grasp,
your death has put its mark upon the mind,
a thought that lingers, waking to itself
with each recurrent impact of your absence,
a pain unfinished now that yours is finished.

A CONFIRMATION

The shadow of a falling leaf
plummeted down the page I read,
as if enlisted for a brief
enactment of what there was said

sadly of dying generations
ceding their glory to the ground.
Foliage, flesh, the pride of nations
pledged to one end. I turned around

too late to see it join the crowd,
the yellow ruck fast thickening.
The lawn was chilled below its shroud.
The pace of loss was quickening.

Of course the stricken world outside
had been destruction-bound for days.
Should words that held me occupied

have better mirrored each grim phase?

Perhaps. I only know it took
the shadow of one casualty
dropping through margins of the book
to bring home fall in full to me.

SEPTEMBER TOADSTOOLS

Fall is their springtime. As the flowers fade
and foresight nudges squirrels to plump their hauls,
and leaves let go, skeletonizing shade,
these flourish, lifting spongy parasols.

Now days turn duller; more and more emerge
out of the dingy trapdoors of the soil,
muscling up along the lawn's damp verge,
burgeoning while the fruits of summer spoil.

Hobnobbing now in squads, in fairy rings,
in straggling queues, lopsided pentacles,
they party on through all the perishings
that set the stage for their conventicles.

A limbless neck, brown gills, and bulbous pate
is no one's notion of a neat profile.
Poisonous, too, most likely. They would rate
low as to virtue, as they do for style.

Give them some points, though, for vitality.
Fed on decay, they get their spores around—

one fresh start, anyway, in this locality
where so much else is dying to the ground.

WINTER STARS

Orion's back. The same old sight:
holding aloft his lion's pelt,
the hunter strides across the night.
His sword, his club, his glittering belt

denote that now, as every year,
that greater belt, the zodiac,
makes room for him and all his gear.
He knows his job—to stay on track

hunting he knows what on the loose
so many light years from the ground.
His shoulder's red with Betelgeuse.
His prey, once more, will go unfound.

Brawnily awesome, not too wise,
he finds the longer nights call forth
in him a lust to roam the skies.
When winds pour fury from the north,

most of the rest of us agree
to stay indoors and let them howl,
enwrapped in comfort such as he
would scorn as he conducts his prowl.

Now, in a night approaching zero,

eyeing the sparklers in his belt,
we'll let him—why not?—play the hero.
When he moves on, the ice will melt.

HANGING ON

Still greening that old lady's door,
the Christmas wreath, when March came round,
was not such out-of-phase décor
as long as snow festooned the ground.

But now the April rains have streaked
the crimson bow a mottled puce.
Needles and all have been antiqued;
exiting winter less than spruce,

it casts more gloom than merriment.
Doesn't she realize, peering out,
the world is halfway into Lent?
Birds are back, cherries about

to blossom, but at her address
it's still Noel. Now passing by,
I think of her at little less
than ninety-five and once more try

to grasp how that must be, and fail.
She teeters out on canes each day
like clockwork to pick up her mail.
Maybe she's let her trappings stay

to show that hurry's out of place,
to stem the rush of feast and fast.
Slowing to something like her pace
I wonder how long this can last.

AN ARRANGEMENT OF DRIED FLOWERS

What was it that our friend said?
"Bad feng shui."
They're off-putting, looking dead
but not all the way.

Odors among which waded
honeybees
are gone from these odd-shaded
arid effigies.

The yellows brought to a halt
short of rust,
the whites brittle as rock salt,
hardened pinks—all must

cast more of a charm on some
audience
that does not regard as glum
would-be permanence.

Give suchlike to the long-range
astronaut,
cabined light years, seeking change

from what time has wrought;

or to kings tucked in stone sar-
cophagi,
whose fine linens daubed with tar
keep their tissues dry.

For us, though, these arrested
blooms inspire
an old thought: time, unbested,
wants each sprig drier.

And who cares to recall that
steady leak
draining softness, scent, all that
even as we speak? ...

NOW WE NOTICE

The rug has faded from the sun's
daily high tides: a background once
as red as blood is brickdust now.
The arabesques of indigo
have traded in their midnight look
for gauzy twilight. All this took
how long? Who wants to count the years?
And even if the rug had ears,
can we reproach it for the way
it let some color ebb each day?
It didn't have a choice: it lay there.
Choosing for now to let it stay there,

we take a dimmer view of light
that rushes colors into sight
in a bright instant, only to
reclaim them as its rightful due
by dribs and drabs, by daily stints
contriving these depleted tints.
More than the sun must be behind
what's happened. Guess the mastermind.
What's left is dignified and wan,
a stoic weft to ponder on,
whose paling pattern represents
the least of time's embezzlements.

III. *A LATE SPRING, AND AFTER*

THE TALLY

Mother first, now my wife.
Dead within a year.
A joke unfunny life
has foisted on me here.

Past sixty, orphanhood
can't be unexpected.
It came; I understood.
Grief was calm, collected.

But that just months ahead

there would be a second
farewell to be said—
that I had not reckoned.

One, two: each blow hit home.
Each left the house more quiet.
Each time, the patient loam
obtained some profit by it.

The orchestra has stopped.
But faintly, unabating
though the baton has dropped,
two notes go on vibrating.

One, two: insistent pair
clinging to every thought.
Murmured to vacant air,
"One, two" adds up to nought.

One, two: the digits can't
supply those fingers' touch
now no more extant,
neither caress nor clutch.

One, two: my footsteps roam
from empty street to street.
Some tireless metronome
sets the relentless beat.

One, two: the pace I keep
requires no grace of art.
Whether I wake or sleep,
despoiled again, my heart

does all it knows to do:
as if it overheard,

it keeps the count—one, two—
will, till I make a third.

WHAT HAPPENED

When the doctor told me that nothing more could be done beyond "making her comfortable," I asked them to bring her home. I was unready, but the house was made ready. She would have to be in the living room, it had the most floor space. We pushed back the sofas, took out the coffee table, rolled up the rug. The Hospice man wheeled in the surprisingly portable hospital bed and set it up in the center of the room, demonstrated all its robotic tilting tricks. Then two gigantic ambulance men brought her up the front steps and in. The nurse soon had her settled.

*

Our son Tony and I took instructions about the oxygen, about the morphine (at first, a dropperful every two hours, then doses closer together as things went downhill at an even faster rate). I grew proficient quickly with the dropper, trying not to think too much about how this now was all that I could do for her. The Hospice promised as much morphine as she needed, which turned out to be just two days' worth.

*

But there was one thing at least still to be done besides giving morphine. The Rector came on the first afternoon and anointed her. We stood by and fumbled through the words, and I felt that something fitting was being accomplished. I watched as the spot on her forehead that I used to kiss received the sign of the Cross.

*

She seemed to know she was home but didn't speak, seemed to be awake but not awake. I had been worried the cats might try to jump up, but they stayed clear, unnerved perhaps by the bed's mechanism, or by the change in her. I kept up a one-sided conversation. They said that hearing was the last thing to go.

*

I had stepped out of the room when Tony called me back: "You better come." She had stopped breathing. Air nestled obligingly about her face but would not be drawn. She looked to be at peace, if lack of expression means peace has been achieved. Every plane and angle of her frail face, motionless on the pillow, imprinted itself unsparingly on my mind. Her gray-green eyes, which always reminded me of the sea-washed pebbles she liked to collect, had turned to a flatter gray. On her left finger were the wedding ring I had given her forty-five years ago and the engagement ring from a few years later (it took a while to afford a ring with a stone). The Hospice nurse removed them and gave them to me, and folded her hands the way they do with dead people in the movies. The undertaker arrived. Tony took me out in the backyard until we heard his van going down the driveway.

*

The remaining stock of morphine could not legally be passed on to another patient. The nurse disposed of it deftly, pouring the vials into a small pile of cat litter, which then was bagged and thrown out. As I watched, I thought crazily: "So no one can get high / On what helped her to die." I called our daughter Catherine in Charleston and began making arrangements.

*

I know, each asterisk seems to say, "And then?" It astonished me that things could just go on happening, to me and around me, after what had happened, could go on as if nothing had happened, as if there were still some point in going on, after my best reason for being was gone out of reach.

*

The same man came back the next day to reclaim the bed. After he wheeled it out, and also collected the oxygen tank and the other things—all this in a matter of fifteen minutes—I stood and looked at the bare stretch of floor, and wondered if it would ever sound right to me, after this, to call it the living room.

A LATE SPRING

She died on Mother's Day.
Our son stood close to me.
What more is there to say?

Spring had just come to stay,
too late for her to see.
She died on Mother's Day,

next to the thin bouquet
he'd gathered hastily.
What more is there to say?

Cold hung on, had its way
down to the last degree.
She died on Mother's Day,

those few flowers on her tray,
buds lagging on each tree.
What more is there to say

now, when the warming clay
seems pleased to let life be?
She died on Mother's Day.
What more is there to say?

THE LOSS OF THE JOY OF COOKING

The book is missing. Somewhere in the house,
misshelved, or at the bottom of some pile,
its columned pages keep their measurements,
ingredients, oven times, and helpful hints
beyond perusal in a fat, useless wad.

The island kitchen counter lets me have
my pick of sides to feel myself marooned on.
I push ahead without a recipe,
halving quantities of what I have
somehow to make edible without
the stir of appetite.

                We used to work
together at it, each on a different side,
she stirring, measuring, tasting, I
chopping, dicing, mincing as required.
Rocking the blade the way she showed me to,
I freed from each raw thing a smell we liked:
the garlic's earthy reek, the ginger's sting,
the anise wisping up from celery leaves.

Now I look at the counter's empty side
and listen to the onion I hacked up
sputtering angrily, intense but futile,
faltering as its fund of hoarded tears
dissolves in the hot oil that some hunks
of meat will sear in next. It probably
isn't quite right (like so much else these days)
but it will do: I need to make it do.

The book is missing. Even if it's found
and followed to the letter, there will still

be loss, the unlisted ingredient,
throwing the best efforts out of balance.
It bakes itself into what's left of life.
The cold plate waits. Nothing now tastes the same.

VOICEMAIL

Well-meaning, tactless, spooked, or simply clueless,
callers wonder why it is still *her* voice
they hear if I'm not there to pick up the phone,
politely asking them to leave a message.
I wish I had an answer, but I haven't.
Am I an archivist, that I should keep
her few seconds of gatekeeping as if
they were historic, like those nip-and-tuck
rescued cylinders from which Tennyson
goes on declaiming, an embattled grandee
sunk deep in time, ravaged by all its static?
(She sounds better than that, if more perfunctory.)
How would she feel? Impatient with my failure
to bring things up to date? People who call
are put off by my failure to "move on."

Once or twice, knowing how crazy it was,
I've dialed my own number just to hear her,
stopping myself short from leaving a message.
I couldn't ask her—could I?—to call me back.
I think the utterly disquieting truth
is that holding her calm voice to my ear
even now feels to me like protection,
and that I fear erasing it would set

a seal for all time on the house's silence,
unbroken now unless I talk to myself.

YOUR HAND

In a house filled with paper I can't go long
without turning up a leaf you'd written on—
an address, a recipe, a list of Things
To Do, many of which escaped getting done,
and now in many cases won't be needed.
I read each scrap as if it were a letter,
realizing how rarely we wrote each other
anything more than refrigerator notes,
living together almost forty-five years.
Even on some old grocery list, creased-up
and come upon in a spring jacket pocket
your hand is firm, incisive, calligraphic,
stroke by stroke set down with an unassuming
elegance. No need for a graphologist
to tell me how true to yourself your writing
was, and remains. I used to enjoy watching
your hand leading the pen in a quick line-dance,
cursive trimly attentive no matter what
trivial matter made you pick up a pen.

Deft characters that inscribed your character.
I wish now I had told you your handwriting
was beautiful, the way I told you sometimes
(not often enough) how beautiful I thought
your hands, both of them, were in every gesture.
I look at oddments of paper and I think:

Your handwriting. Your hand, writing. Your hand.
I think of how my own hand, writing this now,
held your pale hand until it no longer felt
familiar, seized from mine by a colder grip.

CLOCKWORK SONNET

For months on end the clock you gave to me
has sat unwound, deprived of tick and chime.
Somehow I've managed to mislay the key.
My mind sways in a stalemate over time:
Hours, when they were ours, were not hours,
they were unfenced green fields to wander through.
Hours, when there were ours, were not ours
to keep. How can these trite things both be true?

Someday, it may be, if the key is found
I'll do as you would, crank the idle hands
tight for their tut-tut through the daily round.
And we? Will our hands meet when time unhands
me in my turn? Those who claim yes or no
must know something I don't. But time will show.

THE SUN ROOM PLANTS

I water them, and watch as their green lives
give up the ghost for all that I can do.
Without her care it seems that nothing thrives.
They grope for light they lost when she withdrew.

Each root and leaf and intervening stem
weakens without her gift for nurturing.
Could I repot them?—But to look at them
hurts, and confirms they never were my thing.

To them it hadn't mattered much what season
was in control of things beyond the glass.
Their cherished status offered them a reason
to dream their summer had no need to pass.

Dreams cheat me too. Forty-four summers take
leave of me now each morning when I wake.

FLUID OUNCES

Rummaging in a drawer, my fingers felt
something cool and smooth and round—no, ovoid—
which, not too surprisingly, turned out
to be a bottle of her latest perfume.
Heavy for its size, clear glass half full
of a clear liquid. I could look through it
and see the room rendered a bit off-kilter.
I hesitated. Then I opened it.

It smelled like spring, or like spring ought to smell:
light and ferny, lively but elusive.
I thought of her neatly painting on a drop
or two in the soft hollow behind an earlobe,
feeling the cool fragrance meeting her warmth.
I thought of her hand placing the flask where mine
had bumped into it so many months later.

I know where it is now. I can revisit it,
and have, helplessly drawn to this metonymy
two-timing me each time I pick up the scent..
As if a bottle unstoppered were a life
restarted, for a few moments (seconds, really)
it fills the room with figments of her nearness.
Then it fades, lost in the brooding pall
of vacancy that stings the eyes and nostrils
like smoke left over after a house burns down.

THROUGH A GLASS, DARKLY

For someone who didn't make much use of mirrors,
she picked up quite a few of them over the years,
animating bare spaces with mimicking glass.
Each time a new one appeared I would ask, while she
hammered a hook in, "Do we really need that there?"
And she would say, "Look how it makes the room bigger,"
or give as a good reason, "It doubles the light."
She didn't linger in front of any of them.
Even before the grand one above her dresser
she would pause only briefly, tightening earrings,

smoothing a fold, or checking the length of a scarf.
I gave a lot of her scarves to the Hospice Shop.

Grubby with dust I keep forgetting to wipe off,
the dormant glass accepts neglect patiently till
I make the mistake of standing in front of it.
Then I see that her ideas on mirrors, while true,
don't tell the whole story: this one of hers, in what
I still call our bedroom, does make the room bigger,
but does it by making emptiness more pronounced;
it doubles the light, but doubles the darkness too.
And if I look at myself standing in her place
I soon grow sick of my material being,
my helpless casting of shadows, my sham of a
life persisting, my habit of taking up space.

AFTERTHOUGHT

She, above all, enlarged my life and brightened it.
Even now, if I look in memory's mirror
there is some peace to be had when the mind's daylight
defies chronology, finding us side by side,
or cleaving together in the solemnity
of our bodies' worship, and by some great mercy
forgetful of all but time's best gifts and heedless
of any moment beyond the one we were in.

EIGHT MONTHS LATER

A morning early in winter: half asleep,
I lay as I had too often done before,
gulled into thinking life was back to normal.
Then I opened my eyes and when I saw
the bed empty beside me, I knew it wasn't.

I got up even though it was too early.
Sitting down to cold cereal, unrested,
I looked out to see dawn twilight paling.
And it was only by the purest chance
my eyes were raised so as to see the deer,
a young male with a respectable rack
of antlers, crossing over the cleared hill,
pacing out of the woods on the other side,
neither dawdling nor in a great hurry,
merging soon with the stand of trees he aimed for.

I thought of how she would have liked to see this.
We used to watch them together, talking in murmurs,
moved by how much at home they were in the world.
I hadn't seen any lately, grouped or single.
I was just about to push back my chair
when his mate appeared out of the same covert
and walked the path he had pioneered on hard
frostbitten turf, till she too blurred out of view.
Voiceless, he must have stamped, the way they do,
to let her know that it was safe to follow.
With the same measured pace, undeviating,
she had moved as though magnetized to join him.

So: was this an emblem served up with breakfast?
It had some weak points as an analogy,
since in our case she was the first to set out,

while I seem to be waiting for directions.
What I derived from that impassive treeline
was the thought of them out of sight together,
after their crossing of that cold, barren place,
as surely, as invisibly together
as they had been, as they meant always to be.

ENVOY

How shall I save my words from growing faint
In their attempt to summon back the same
Long sunlit hours that once were yours and mine?
All cast in shadow now? Not if complaint
Rewords itself to praise. Graced with your name,
Your musing glow, light quickens every line.

IV. *FERRYING*

BY THE POND

Dragonflies dart, basking turtles doze.
Noon is furnishing
water with a trance that grows

       deep from daily burnishing.

Passersby who automatically
       give slime a bad name
    should slow down, see what I see.
    It might nudge them to reframe

received opinions. At the pond's edge
       turbid sepia
    sprawls unlovely from the sedge
    to meet what seems to be a

fabulous floating green mantilla—
       spun of such a shade
    as if one might distill a
    thready essence out of jade

or other swag equally precious,
       then wide-cast a net
    of it, close-woven, lustrous,
    each intense diatom set

gemlike, snug among gemlike fellows.
       The Great Smaragdine
    Tablet (raft-borne, I suppose)
    might fling out a sheen as fine,

vibrant with the workings of the sun
       that keeps giving hints
    of fire fused in every one
    of these algae pooling glints.

Yes, if you insist: a trick of light.
       But so too are all
    favors caught and prized by sight
    that prodigal sun lets fall.

PATHS CROSSING

Careering composedly over the road before us,
with a purposeful lope and pennant of rust-red tail,
accustomed to getting there fast, without any fuss
(*there* being now a weed patch abutting the county jail),

the fox, having come at a bound out of nowhere, regained
his invisibility thanks to the snarl of scrub
that so imperturbably took him in headlong. We strained
our eyes in vain for an encore, then gave them a rub

of wonderment as you might after seeing the streak
of a meteor darting through space: while not celestial,
this dash of his featured a gravity-taunting technique
that shaped a series of springs into something less bestial

than balletic. There wasn't a chance to applaud him, though—
he'd raced off into his otherness, and we had places to go.

NEWS ITEM

Five thousand red-winged blackbirds,
oddly aloft at night,
got flight directions backwards
in this, their final flight.

Even as they were winging
their way across the sky
some force possessed them, flinging

them down to earth, to die.

On New Year's Eve they bought it.
And the macabre scene
was such that people thought it
prefigured Halloween.

A kamikaze action?
A bow to Newton's Law?
Still, no great satisfaction
to folks in Arkansas.

The town of Beebe starred in
the news—no more ignored,
with every lawn and garden
hosting the fallen horde.

Their mourner: one sad phoebe.
No lowering of flags.
The citizens of Beebe
got out their garbage bags.

Far more than four-and-twenty,
and none alive to sing,
they left us groundlings plenty
of cause for pondering.

If we were ancient, Roman,
and worried over Fate,
we might call this an omen.
We might haruspicate.

We won't. But still, we wonder,
made restless in our beds
by the night skies we're under,
by what's above our heads.

SENSITIVE PLANT

(*Mimosa pudica*)

Though it may look as self-possessed
as any plant safe in a pot,
this one is different from the rest.
Most of them trust me. This does not.

Its feathery leaf, a leaf all fringe,
will at my inadvertent touch
collapse into a total cringe,
fold up to hug itself in such

a visceral flinch I jerk away
myself, outmastered by surprise.
How it mimes *Noli me tangere*
with muscles none to galvanize

is for a botanist to explore.
(It should be hardier, you'd think,
transplanted from a forest floor.)
But I, abashed to see it shrink,

begin to think of other creatures,
sentient or not, unequally
equipped with such defensive features.
How many have been jarred by me,

meandering past, with inattention
blurring the bounds in which I live?
More victims than I care to mention.
Which of us now is sensitive?

HER MOTHER'S SEASHELL

sat on the bedside table, almost
as big as the black phone next to it.
Each week she could count on being called
to talk long distance to grandparents
and didn't need to be told, when at
loose ends, to pick up the shell and press
her ear close to it, as to a more
primitive receiver, listening
to what was said to be the ocean
going about its restless business.
(That was long distance, too: the nearest
beach was two states away.) The sea voice
was neither daunting nor alluring,
just white noise emitted like a drift
of air escaping an unmapped cave.
Always there for her, the sound announced
itself in that marine dial tone,
more an inarticulate prelude
than a message delivering sense.
In any case, the shell, to look at,
did not strike her as being like
a mouth itching to chat. The smooth pink sheen
devolving back into its hidden
labyrinth was more convincingly
an ear waiting for her to whisper
back to it something private, a secret.
She never did, though, having a child's
too keen sense of what would be silly.
It was years later she thought of this
and wondered what she could have told it,
couched in terms it might be in tune with—
Sometimes I feel flung up by the tide
or *Sometimes I feel empty inside?*

Too late now, though, to experiment.
The shell was gone, shattered by someone's
slapdash dusting. It would have listened
in calm, mother-of-pearl inertia,
yielding back its never-ending sigh.

TRANSFORMATION SCENE

The days go slowly but the years go fast.
Old movies used to bridge the story's gaps
by morphing falling leaves to frantic snow,
or showing pages from a massive book
madly flipping themselves, or, desperately,
superimposing on the hapless background
an hourglass turning cartwheels. When the cast
came back after such intervals, their costumes
were updated, their erstwhile raven tresses
were streaked with white, or thinned, or salt-and-peppered.
It was crude, but what else could they do,
collapsing decades into ninety minutes?
The dents and scuffs that time supposedly
had put upon those celluloid personae
were in the end no harder to believe
than what the forward tug of time had done
to maim or to refine their inner selves,
as the remaining reel was left to show.

You think of this when the old friend turns up
after how many years you can't remember,
and each of you feels awkwardly confronted,
making what you hope is not too blatant

an inventory of the other's features
that do or don't fit the remembered image.
Any dissimulation, though, is wasted;
you're both as obvious in your intent
as cats competing in a staring match.
Once recognition stifles disbelief,
it seems you each still have a part to play.
You're on! By now it's too late to be asking
where and when you might have come by a script.

FERRYING

We took that ferry ride too many times.
It was a way to shave an hour off
the trip, less of a grind than the Expressway.
But it was boring, and the only way
to put up with it was to ritualize it.
So, with the car stowed in what I guess
would not, on ferry boats, be called the hold,
we stood on deck and watched the concrete pier
receding, watched where we had been get small.
We felt the engine's hum more than we heard it.
Something kept us determined to look back
until land disappeared, and this at last
was like an upper and a lower lid,
sky and water, gradually colluding
until the rickety, unlovely port
was gone as if our own eyes closed on it.
Then for a short time there was only water
lapping away on all sides, nothing yet
apparent as a haven in the offing—

so we noticed, turning about face. Somehow
we never felt as drawn to that so-far-
unspotted destination as we'd been
to what we had seen vanish. At midpoint,
the ferry's twin passed by us with a hoot,
chugging to where we'd come from, as if both
boats were hauled along by a double pulley.

Car fumes, boat fumes, just a slim whiff of salt;
blasé occasional seagulls, more than occasional
children bickering, parents buying them soda.
We must have felt at least a dim unease
at the hiatus that our fare had paid for;
we kept close to each other the whole time.
The water now was army-colored, empty
except for the odd sailboat in the distance,
and except for our own cargo of noise
the Sound was largely silent.

                        It's been years
since I have driven on or off that boat.
Now when it swashes into my dreams, it's all
much as it was on the vibrating deck
except that I'm alone and facing forward,
for a change having become impatient
to see what hasn't yet come into view.
All around me wrinkles that sullen water
we got across so often in one piece,
even emptier now than I remember.
I always wake before shore is in sight.

WINTER SUNSET

Veiled by a winter scrim
of early evening haze,
the sun gives but a dim
impression of its blaze,

barren of rays, a disc
of crimson trundling west,
peered after without risk
by eyes not seared but blessed

by what pours without stint
on ground clenched tight with cold:
rose, purple, pink, each tint
touched at its edge with gold.

Could there be more to see?
Replacing each bold swatch
comes twilight's clarity.
It is for that I watch:

when, in a moment's trance,
viewer and viewed are one.
Earth itself seems to glance
back after day just done.

The year '15 retires.
In '16 so will I.
Surveying these banked fires
beneath a darkening sky,

I'd say this landscape frames
hints of how best to go.
Others may crash in flames.
My goal is afterglow.

NOTES

"Morning Song": This was written at the request of my friend and colleague, the composer Allen Bonde. His setting of the piece is for voice (soprano) and piano.

"Last Days in Camden": This poem was written and first published in 1992, marking the centennial of Walt Whitman's death. Apart from those taken from Whitman's writings, quotations are from early biographical sources.

"An Exhumation": The italicized lines are quoted from two sonnets ("The Lamp's Shrine" and "Life-in-Love") in Rossetti's sonnet sequence, *The House of Life*.

"Drowned Towns": Many of the facts in this poem are drawn from two books by J. R. Greene: *The Creation of Quabbin Reservoir* and *The Day Four Quabbin Towns Died*, both published by The Transcript Press, Athol, Massachusetts. Other material was derived from informational booklets available at the Quabbin Visitors' Center.

"The Poe Toaster Prepares for His Annual Visit": The late-night birthday visits to Poe's grave, as described here, were begun by an anonymous devotee sometime before being first reported in print in 1950, and continued for decades. They were carried on in later years by another, presumably the first visitor's son. The last such visit to be observed took place in 2009. The ritual was still being performed annually when this poem was written.

"A Spirit Photograph: W. B. Yeats and Another": For this image, see R. F. Foster, *W. B. Yeats: A Life, vol. I: The Apprentice Mage, 1865-1914* (New York: Oxford University Press, 1997), Plate 31.

"Old Man of the Mountain": This rock formation—the Great Stone Face, as Nathaniel Hawthorne called it—was a longtime attraction for sightseers in the White Mountains. Some early viewers of the profile were reminded of Thomas Jefferson. It appears as the state symbol on the back of New Hampshire's Statehood Quarter. In the early morning of May 3, 2003 it collapsed in pieces, irreparably.

"In Storage: A Calder Cat": This wood sculpture by Alexander Calder, ca. 1930, not invariably exhibited, is in the collection of the Yale University Art Gallery.

"The House of the Tragic Poet": This building, one of the villas of Pompeii buried in the eruption of Vesuvius in 79 CE, was so named by modern archeologists because of its numerous frescoes depicting scenes from Greek mythology, and mosaics, one of which depicts actors preparing for a performance. The house was excavated in 1824.

A Late Spring, and After: My wife died on May 11, 2014. The poems in this section were written between January and August, 2015.

"By the Pond": The Great Smaragdine Tablet, also called the Emerald Tablet, is a brief Hermetic text whose earliest (sixth to eighth centuries) source is in Arabic. It was translated into Latin in the twelfth century and was thereafter intently studied by alchemists, including Isaac Newton, who made his own English translation of it. It speaks forcefully and cryptically of the unity of all things and propounds the doctrine of correspondences: in Newton's rendering, "that which is below is like that which is above & that which is above is like that which is below to do the miracles of one only thing." W. B. Yeats alludes to the Tablet and especially to this assertion in the second of his "Supernatural Songs." In my own poem, the phrase "the workings of the sun" echoes part of the Tablet's final sentence.

CPSIA information can be obtained
at www.ICGtesting.com
Printed in the USA
LVHW052021010422
715081LV00004B/33